To all of those who are special to me with love.

Most of all to my children.
I hope my travels will give you light for a better
future. Don't give up on your dreams.
I am just a parent and I am not perfect but I hope that
I can give you the inspiration to follow your dreams and
never tell yourself you can't do it. You have the best
chance to change the world - no matter how small of a
change you have made.

Love Dad

Simple Thoughts to ponder on

The Adult Story Book

By Fortunet L Wilson

© 2011 Fortunet L. Wilson, Berlin, (New Jersey)
Production and Publishing House: Books on Demand GmbH, Norderstedt

ISBN 9-7838-4480-874-2

Contents

This book it is based on random thought and it should be read with an open mind. I will take pictures and use them as a reference to open avenues to new ideas and ways of thinking. I am not a very good artist but I try. I plan to give you the words behind my view of these pictures that I hope will energize new ways of looking at life and yourself. There is no wrong or right and it is more of a philosophy setting then a fact finding adventure; but if this wakes up that part of you in which you want to travel on, please walk on either path, the invitation is there.

Sometimes we go through life with a lot of "what if's?" and most of the time they go empty and never pursued. Reading this book should give you a chance to look at this question and follow through. This book could be the perfect window to meet new friends share thought and truly inspire energy which could lead to solving world problems, curing a deadly disease, or simply just give you new ideas to relook on old subjects that you always wanted to review.

I have my opinion and yes they are opinions, and if this sparks a nerve then the book is working for you. Some of my opinions will be a bit disturbing to some but I want to reassure you that I am not some far left or right fanatic on a mission to conquer the world; I may touch on some subjects that are not so popular with the world, but as I said in the beginning: open your mind to look at these subjects and give them an impartial view and be evaluated from all angles to figure "your right and your wrong". This is what I am striving for and I hope after you finish this book, you can be the inspiration for the next.

Please do not be scared or discouraged if you find a subject that bothers you. This is why it is written, because these subjects are the information that you, and just as well as your children will encounter. It is better to explore the sections then it is to shut you off from them so you can grow and have courage tackle the hard questions and thoughts that are brought before you. This is not a religious cult driven writing; it is a reflection of society and what is moving through the cables of the "Modern Library" of the world. All of these subjects were found on the internet - all I did was: add a twist. What will you find?

I really hope you enjoy reading my book and I hope that in the end you will be looking for more. I had a lot of fun writing it, and I hope you will have a lot of fun reading it is well. So have fun, enjoy the dialogue and energize your mind to do, what you never thought it could do.

"TOO EASY"

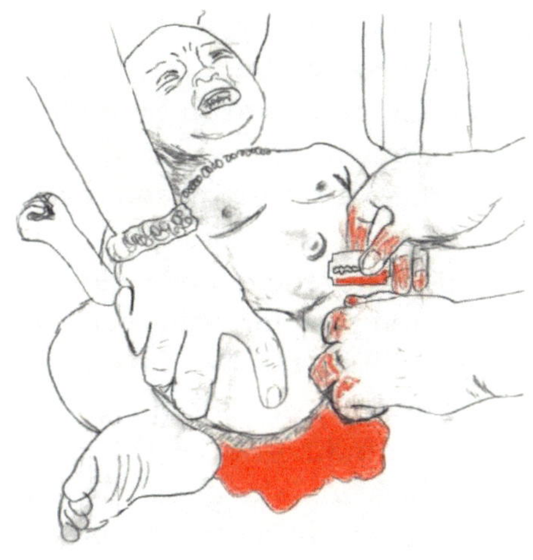

She will never know because her family said so.

She will never be given a chance because of a cruel and vicious act. This practice has a long and dark history and yes it still goes on all over the world in some dark corner or at the end of most villages of the Central African continent as well as Indonesia and some parts of the border of Iraq and Iran as well as regions in the Kazakhstan regions. She was a victim through fate and the ignorance of her culture; all because some group of men did not want her to feel the beautiful sensations that come with love and copulation.

Days before this moment she was happy she played in the yard she lived what could be a normal and happy life. She was deceived by her mother, her grandmother and by the order of her father because of her sex; she had to pay for a crime she had never committed. The mother dresses her up in the ceremonial dress or in some cases just lied to her on what she perceived to be a day in the market. These elderly women are so brainwashed into this insanity that to them it's normal, and this little one has no clue.

She is brought to the female elder's hut, or room where they sing and they make her feel: today is going to be special and it will be the best, she had had in her life. They gather around her and all of a sudden they pin her down... Now her grandmother or the village female elder pulls out the razor blade, the glass, the knife, or whatever cuts well; and she slowly severs the outer tissue away as the girl screams in agony and the women cheer that the act has been complete. Once it is cut away she has to feel the piercing of the needle as it is punctured into the vaginal region to make the virginal passage smaller. As the thread runs through the punctured hole and as it burns due to the running of the thread in the inter flesh of her vaginal area. It is slowly sealed just small enough so that all she can do is urinate and release her menstrual residue. All of the joys, all of the passion are now being slowly sealed because of some sick culture feels that a woman is only here for three reasons: To have sex, to have babies, to manage the house when he is gone.

The women will later convince her that it is ok and soon she will be all right. She will then go through life, until she finds a mate, whom the family has already arranged to be united with. She may not love him, but she may never know how to love him, because she has lost the only connection of completing their union to love her man.

When he lays her down and spread her legs with no sentiments of compassion; he will thrust into her and she has to re-live the same experience she has went through years ago. As he thrust and thrust, she will feel no joy, she will not feel no passion, no fireworks, no emotions, just this penis moving in and out of her. She will never cherish this moment, she will never sit with the girls, as she would have explained this moment, and she will never feel any passion for this man. She will only feel that it's her duty to live under the commands and demands of this man, whom deep inside she will never learn how to love. She will only know pain and duty to a cause, which should have been lost eons ago.

This is the result of no education, no sense of respect, derivative of religious belief and the commitment to dominate the weak.

You have to stop thinking that your world is similar to the ones who live their lives around you. Each of us has a different past from the next. You have to stop thinking that what you live through life, others live the same as you. Ask this little girl, if she is happy because of a passive society, and I'm sure you will not like the answer. Be aware of the events around you, become aware of what you are passing by.

Make it so that our society will not come to acts like this for a sense of empty values.

What We See.

I am a good man. I can make my own calls. I can take on the world single handed, I am unstoppable. I woke up one morning and for reasons I will never know; I joined the military and see where it will go. I learned new things, climbed new heights, did things I never thought, I could do. They taught me how to be all I could be. In my eyes I considered myself the king of the hill, but to the world I was all but a little boy, wet behind the ears, a baby in a cradle, still to be nursed by the mother of life. I stood and walked in the rain, I stood and walked in the snow, and there was no place I could not go. I went to war. I preserved peace. I did things, no normal man could do.

Through these lessons I was prepared to be all I could be; but they never prepared me for Germany...

I got off the plane and what did I see? This 5ft 8in beauty looking at me... She came to me, could you believe it? To me, and wanted to know more about me; but little did I know that I was just fresh meat for her to gobble me up like a treat.

All I could think was: WOW, this beautiful flower wants to know me, a little tiny leaf on a tree. She shows me all that Germany has to offer. She makes me feel, like there was no other, but me. Little that I knew that my brothers before me went through her like last week's dirty laundry. She made me feel good. She said, it was me, she will adore, but in her absence, her friends would call her continuously a whore. This meant nothing to me. I thought I had captured an excellent score. I thought she was mine for evermore.

Then one day her "Boo" came back and this is a fact, and all of a sudden I was on the curb, trying to get my dignity back.

This is where another beast is born and also when men are transformed, and now I walk like a beast in the night, looking for these creatures for my delight, and when I travel in my disguise, the only thing that fills our eyes is just: how fast I can lay on you and get between your thighs. This for some may seem crazy and for some, it may be true.

So we ask ourselves what you would do. Look at yourself. You know, who you are. Why can't you be ladies and not some kind of porn or music video superstar? He knows a good lady and he knows a good fuck, so I say to you ladies: "What's the heck is up?" Stop standing by, come to your sisters, when you hear their cry. Teach her dignity, teach her respect, and show her that a man can be kept. You let us do the things we do because at the end of the day, when we go home, we know, she won't give it up until I say "I do". So when you are out and about, think of what your sisters have done to make this beast come out. Behind every player, there is a broken heart.

Bring us back and give us a fresh start, let us be the men you deserve to have in your heart. You know what is right and what is wrong; be honest with yourself and be honest to the ones around you. If you want a baker, go to the bakery. If you want a preacher, go to a church. If you want a player, go to the sports field. If you want a dog, go to the dog house. For goodness sake, don't blame the man, when you came to his environment to play.

This is a mad circle and needs to end. Guys; wake up and realize what you do. I have one for you too, but it is not the next page. Keep reading.

Keep it real; it works better when you do this.

Is it really this way, when she is upset?

Well guys, I think you can relate to this one. Yes you are the little knight here and the odds seem to be against you. Is this how it feels, when you and your woman have a fight? Does it seem like she always has the upper hand on it all the time? Well there is a solution to this issue: it's called communication. Yes, this is very difficult for some of us and it is a skill, you should learn to use well. Most of the time she just wants to be noticed, too bad it is always during the game or your favorite episode of a series or during the time you are trying to get to that next level of that favorite video game of yours. Yes it always seems like bad timing, doesn't it?

Well, when this happens, you need to be aware that she hates it when you love or like something more than her. She wants to be the center of your world and nothing is supposed to be in the way. Most women love attention and they need this in their own special way.

Guys, we know that we love them, we know that they are our jewels, but neither evolution nor the Supreme Being blessed us with telepathic powers; and yes it is necessary that we have to use our mouths sometimes to show we care.

Yes it's hard... The truth is always important and yes it is in your interest to use it as much as you can. You have to use it, because when you lie, this picture can become very familiar to you and you will have a lot to answer for when it is all done. She does not have to know everything but you have to give her enough to calm down, so you can enjoy the finer things in life. Women are the most intriguing creatures and do yourself a favor, don't try to figure out their reasoning because you will never be right. As you move along, you will find that it is rare you have a good idea and the good ideas you have are only, because she agrees and has thought of the same thing as you at this time.

There is no absolute, when you are dealing with them, except that there is "no absolute" when you are figuring out this equation. "Yes" is not always yes and "No" is not always no, and it is easy to get in trouble, when you do not analyze carefully. The only time "no" really means "no" is, when you two are discussing sex. Guys our law is NO MEANS NO. You will be granted immunity, when you take this at its face value. It will save you a lot of hard ache.

For everything else: heck, play with it, tweak it to your tolerance level. Find what works for you. There is no true right but there are plenty of wrongs. Stand your ground; because sometimes you have to be an asshole, they will not admit it but they like this from time to time. Many of them don't want a wimp and they smell fear a mile away. Did you ever wonder why girls always fall for the bad boys? It's because being a bad boy arouses them. They don't like to admit it, but the bad boys do have their women longer then good boys; bad boys just know when to be bad.

This was just to give you a different view and hopefully you may not have to break out the armor so much, when you think out of the box.

The new poison the new bad word.

Yes there was a time, when we were the masters of our universe, we had no bounds and we had no boundaries, and now look at us approximately 200 years later: and we are compared to most third world countries. Who's to blame? You may not want to hear this, but it is only us to blame. We did this to ourselves, we stopped being Americans and this is sad to see. These are just a few areas, I would like to touch on to understand, where I am coming from.

Government: They just gave up, they sit in congress and they let Wall Street run us in the hole of debt, they do not hold business's feet to the fire and regulate their criminal acts. They send us to wars, which make no sense, they line their pockets monetarily and they leave the

20

common man to the wolves of finance. They freeze the wages of their employees and they let countries about the size of Rhode Island push them around. They are more worried about the misconduct of members on the internet then they are about whether we will be a country in the future. They fight constantly against productivity and they never come to a solution. They have forgotten what The Constitution stands for and they continue to let us fall. They strive to fix the world's problems and they forget about their own back yard. They cut our pensions, because they will never need it, when they are old. They screw up our health care, because they have enough money in their pocket to never depend on it. They are forgetting the common man, the one who put them there in the first place.

Teachers: They loss the will to teach; they fail to give us inspiration; they cease to give us the knowledge to build our nation to be what it once was. If they would have taught these points to government members, on how important it is to have knowledge and wisdom, they would not had to worry about being pushed to the side like they are now. Compared to most minimum wage jobs in the economy, they have to struggle to make ends meet. They have the power to teach our children how important it is to make programs that will support them and they just treat their job like a paycheck and a means of survival instead of a time to enrich our children with the knowledge to succeed. Where would we be without them? There are only a few left who teach real lessons and the system is pushing them out. We see this now as they are being laid off for the sake of reducing debt.

Parents: We lost the will to love our children 100%, because we are too worried about how we will feed them food instead of knowledge. We are the ones who created these monsters, because we had little to no values to live by. Each and every member in this institution has had a mother or a father and due to the deterioration of our values we set the examples of what our children have done as they debate whether we should live or die when we are too old to function. We have taught our kids to treat us as a liability instead of an asset. We taught them to push us to the side and not listen to the knowledge we have to share, when they need it the most. We now are faced with a future that may not have a happy ending. We forgot who we are and what we stand for. Yes it hurts and some of you have tried, but the masses rule and we have lost our voice in our society.

Wake Up.

What happen to this institution? Why do they consistently dumb down our nation with information that has no relevance? It seems like it is more a resemblance of a reality show then an information tool. Where did the real stories go? Media today is more of a propaganda tool then a true creditable institution that it once was. Here we are the panicle of free speech and it seems more like they are only promoting the highest bidder's view, when it comes to what is said and what is not.

Why should we have to worry about the teenage pop star's birthday, what does that have to do with real news? What is so important about the prime time celebrity's divorce? Why is it that actors are treated like politicians and politicians are treated like actors? Why does a talk show host have more political influence then a candidate?

They can get away with this, because America loves happy endings and they love to run away from the truth, their problems and them self's. They claim that it is depressing to hear bad news all the time. Well why run away from it then. Our country gives us the power to change it and we all just cower in our corners and say "it's not my problem".

This is wrong, we would rather run to the next box office hit then run to a voting closet. We would more likely gather for a Hot Dog eating contest than a town hall meeting. We are slowly retracting to isolationism. The media promotes this every day. Words are backed by money and power and not true virtues. They are sessional one sided drones only, because the ratings from a select few, whom are chosen to represent the other 300 million, who also are in the top 1% of the financial earning sector tell us how to live our life. One day we are all supposed to hate whites and the next we hate blacks and when we get bored of both we hate Latin Americans until the next issue. We always see non-whites associated with crime and poverty and we see whites associated with serial killers and white collar crime. Then when it starts to seem like a pattern is forming, they throw in the "trailer trash" to give it character.

Well are you mad yet?

Where did real news in America go? It is sad that that our own Secretary of State recognizes that our media is going down the drain. We were advised that news coming out of Russia and some Arabic regions are more resourceful than our own and that we better get with the program with real issues. I may sound racist and I am not but this is what captivates Americans more than real issues. The media should be ashamed of their selves.

The nation feels that news parodies are more resourceful then our main news centers. The hosts of these parodies admit this is entertainment and we still take their word for being the truth. Sounds like we are confused right? It seems like the host on our news programs would rather bash their guest than let the news be seen from both sides of the issues. World news only gets approximately five minutes of air time and the rest is on bashing policies instead of discussing the repercussions of what these policies can affect. Experts on issues are treated like little kids, while the news host appears to know more on the subjects than they really do.

The only real news is the weather in America right now; the rest; well you decide.

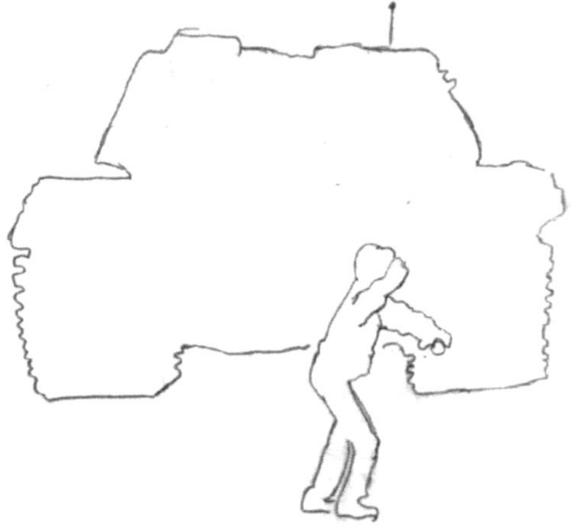

You have to love kids; they seem to always put their selves in some interesting situations. Parents sometimes forget just how adventurous they can really get. You should be happy, if you did not have to worry where they are and what they are doing. If children can think it then they can believe in it; and this picture could be the result. Take the time to insure that you teach your children, how to approach problems. This is why the world is the way it is, where some are taught well and some are left with loose ends. It's great to give your children dreams and hope for a future and no doubt education is the key; with children you have to be careful, because what you think is perceived as advice is related to the last cartoon they watched, and life is somehow related to this cartoon and your child will be in a situation almost like the young man and this battle tank.

Children are a treasure, not a bargaining chip. You have the first say for the first 18 years of their lives. Use this time wisely to make our future a better place. You can see the result of what parental failure has done. Just look at the world today. It's not about being rich or being poor, it's about a comfortable way of life.

The greatest mistake we ever did was to own something. This is the real route of evil, not money because money was just a derivative of what has happen to the world. This is why in some parts of the world they waste, because they have too much and the other parts they starve, because they have too little. Isn't it crazy that metal, paper, rocks and plastic are more important than fruits, vegetables, meat and shelter? Wars are the result of parent's hate, greed, selfishness and fear. We are all guilty in some way. It was parents, who taught us the difference of skin. It is parents, who taught us, how to give up on our dreams. It's the parents, who taught us, how to horde all of our possessions for a "better future". Are we just stuck teaching our children, how to survive, or are we teaching them, how to live? There is a fine line in this question but it has worth.

The parents have taught the leaders of today how to destroy lives, how to possess all they can accumulate and how to dumb down society and others to passively exist, so they can get their share and move on. This is also contagious, because good children can turn bad as well. Why is a person a racist? They either think, they are better then or they fear the races around them. Whose fault is that? Parents do not always think of the repercussions of their teachings.

Parents sometimes forget that they may have a future person of power in their mist. Greedy parents always regret, when their greedy children cast them into the waste land. Good parents never see a senior citizens home and are never a burden to their children, because they paid attention when their children needed them the most. They coached them into the right direction and their children provided a future for all. Selfish parents have to deal with selfish kids and regret, when they steal all of their possessions. Passive parents have spoiled children, who never learn to take care of them self, they always want to play. Protective parent's children are the first to go, because they never had to defend them self. Ignorant Parents have it the worse (blind leading the blind).

What is your impact on your children?

Be a soldier, it's a great opportunity, we will educate you, and we will provide you with all your needs. All you have to do is pledge a legions to our empty but profitable cause. We have the best medical program, free money for college, we can show you a whole new way of life. The possibilities are endless and it's all for you. We will give you orders, which make no sense. We will bully you, because these $0. 95 patches on our chess say we can. We will brain wash you on empty values, and we will not give you a sense of worth, if you do not listen. Your superiors will use you for their own interest, isn't that great? If it hurts you, who cares? We will send you to a doctor, who really does not care for you, because if they make a mistake, they do not have to be responsible for their actions and it will take years, before we compensate you for their mistake. When you get old or fat or you think "Out of the box", we will kick you out, turn our backs on you and find the next idiot to take your place. Come on and join us, it's a great life.

This is uncomfortable to hear, but countries desert their veterans. They leave them in the dust and they pray that they disappear from their society. Once you walk out the door, that's it. Prisoners have more rights than soldiers in some countries. What have we gained? Nothing... The skill that you have learned has no relevance at all when you leave the military. All of your accomplishments are oblivious to the ones you fought for. Honor, very little, you will only get this if you're lucky. Your own government makes it difficult to support your family, if you go. So you stay for as long, as you can to retire; and in the end they tax your benefits for giving up your life and way of life to your country. Their weapons and equipment are more useful to your superiors than your wellbeing. They push you out of the door and you hope it does not slam you in the ass when you go.

Remember, you are your diplomat's last solution for resolve. Also remember, you are a number and not a person. Make your resume your "Mona Lisa" from day one in the service; this means record all of your accomplishments and network where ever you go, this means soldiers and civilians around the military. Stats and reports have a higher precedence then your training and wellbeing. They will rob from you and leave you in the dust. Team work is gone, it's all about you; this is what they will show you. If you want to make a difference, get out and become a leader like a President or Prime Minister or maybe a member of congress or parliament.

Don't forget our brothers in arms. Most Veterans who make it big in society often do. If you are a superior, teach your subordinates how to function. Teach them how to win. Teach them how to come home. Teach them how to be productive members of society. Teach them how to love their deity, their self, their family and their country and its citizens. We fight, so you have the right to live. We fight, so you have the right to speak. So when that citizen walks up to you and tries to destroy your character and ridicule you just tell them "your welcome" because you gave your citizens the right to do so, when your blood was shed on the battle field.

Most of military members could care less what happens to you and they will forget that you exist, when you leave their squad, company, brigade or division.

The answer was here all the time.

You break the game out, you set up the pieces and you and your grandfather sit in the living room and begin to play. You play and you play for hours on in but you lose. Your grandfather smiles and says "You will learn some day". So you practice a bit and you build confidence and you challenge your grandfather again. You play for hours on in and you almost got him, but out of the blue he pulls a fast one and you lose again. So now you become obsessed and you learn and you study, because you know, the next time you will do all you can do to win. You do this for the next two months. Finally you come to that day; you challenge your grandfather again. Play for hours on in and this time you win. Mad and upset to give his last dollar away he puts it in your hand and he looks you in the eye. He says "My child you finally learned the game, but now here's the real lesson." He sips his tea and he says

"Now It all ends up back in the box." He continues: "All those hotels, all that money, all that land was really never yours and in the end, it all goes in the box... Players will come and go and you will be forgotten; the game will go back on the shelf, waiting for the next group of players. " It will all go back in the box in the end.

Think about it....

Take this game and examine it. Then look at the global economy and I am sure, you will see a very close resemblance of this game that has been around for years. Do you think that the money in your pocket is worth its true value? Guess again, because all of it is debt. Yes debt. Your currencies value died in the 70's when they ended the use of the gold standard. This allowed the banks to print as much currency as they wanted.

China did this and the people needed wheel barrels of their currency, just to buy a bag of rice in the past. Today we see the result of this action and the world's economies suffer. Fake money for real goods: that's the trend of the times, sick isn't it? We buy debt we sell debt, this is called the stock market and when you review the rules of this game; remember "The Bank never goes broke." Yes the bank never goes broke. This means that you can use scrap paper to buy and sell goods; we call this bonds and shares. Banks take countries, find an individual and manipulate this individual to the top of the higher echelons of government, corporatize their assets and run them to the point that they ask the international banks for loans and they are trapped in interest rates and inflation.

The sad part is that before the people feel the worse part of this concept, it's too late. Once they get in the countries roots, they dumb the people down with reality TV and news on the pop stars lives, they fail to address world issues and then the point of implosion has begun.

So keep doubting it, play stupid, stay the way you are and your toilet paper will be worth more than your currency. All of this has happened before and it will all happen again.

Just remember, it all goes back in the box....

From the beginning you are taught to go to school, get good grades, so you can get an education and find a good college.

Yeah right...

College is the biggest scandal in the modern world. It is just as bad as the bank scandal. Children these days pursue worthless degrees and in the end they can't even get a job. Children are not taught, how to start a business, how to buy gold and other precious metals, how to read the stock market and thinking out of the box. Our colleges are more interested in beautiful landscapes and heated pools, the list goes on. The old "High School Jock" makes more money than the professor teaching science. Yeah the sports coach, get it? Teachers do not have the opportunity to teach.

All we are producing are drones, who are walking into the oven of the American crisis. If you disagree, then look around; if our colleges were so great, do you think we would be in a great deficit we are having now? Would we have Congressmen who can't get their head out of the rear end to run the country? Would our country be among the unhealthiest in the world? We refuse to teach our children and we give foreign students the red carpet to knowledge. They go home and later buy our country out, because we can't count or manage our own assets. Do you know what a derivative is? Do you know what a commodity or blue chip is? If this sounds weird to you then guess what? You are behind.

They give children with no financial stability; a loan that is more than most houses on the market. They get deeper and deeper in debt to the point they can never pay it back. The average university student in the past had a debt of around $2000 and now a student today has almost 100,000 or more. Sick isn't it? The kid who learns a trade has a better future than a doctor or a lawyer. We tell our kids to get white collar jobs and the result: No farmers, no mechanics, no truck drivers, well you get it. You spend four to six years in a university just to get a part time job that is not even close to your degree that you studied for. We are depending on the stock market to save the day well. If you think this is the way, good luck. You are the most ignorant being, our species has ever created. How are you going to eat, who is going to make the designer labels that we flaunt on the sidewalk? Yeah China, India, Vietnam can do it. They get rich as we get poor.

Wait until our currency is no longer the world's reserve, well... Can you say crash and burn? Thanks to most of our colleges a graduate's of this institution, we are going in the ground. It is all just one big Ponzi scheme waiting to collapse. Parents: is it not sad that you can do your children's homework up to the 12 grade level? Aren't they supposed to teach us? Is it not sad that your child's education is worth more them of the houses on the market?

Well, I guess it's all good for you because you have more important things to do and that's feed them non-nutritional foods right? Well it does not take too much to give your child the time and knowledge to learn from your mistakes. Talk to them and show them the way. Give them the tools they need to survive and live.

Advice...

Go to the internet, learn it, it's all out there; you have so much information to learn from and you use this tool only for communication and entertainment. Wake up get those children on this tool and prepare them for life not a worthless piece of paper.

Educate yourself, before you have to learn the hard way.

Moms are the most powerful creatures on the planet. They can change nations with a glare; they can cure every cut with their saliva. They can cook anything on the planet and make it taste good. Mothers are excellent psychologists. They know you inside and out. Mothers can leap tall buildings in a single bound. Mothers can do all and be all - and in some cases see all. They truly are the most powerful beings on the planet. They even can create life with a little help. Such powerful creatures have the capacity to rule the world. We are taught to respect them, to listen to them and to honor them.

Such strength and power and they still submit to the world and its ways. Some mothers teach their children to be powerful and survive; they teach you to put yourself ahead of all the rest. Unfortunately they do not give the full lesson. When these lessons are taught the good way, we have children, who help humanity. They cure diseases, they teach and educate the weak, and they lead for the good of mankind and the elements around them. When they are not given the full lesson, you have war strife and poverty. Some mothers being deprived by their mother try to live their live through their children. This is dangerous, because in the end they are left in the cold. Other mothers give their children the opportunity to grow and appreciate life; they are rewarded with all the benefits of their child's knowledge.

There are good mothers, bad mothers, desperate mothers and stupid mothers - all the result of mothers. Mothers must understand if they have not already, that children are our future and they have a big influence in their life. They are the givers of life and we take this for granted. Mothers do what they have to do and every mother has her story. If society allows, show your children a reasonable way for all to benefit in this age. Do the best you can, to create a positive way of thinking. Don't abandon them, don't give them away and expect twenty years later to ask for their forgiveness. You should have been there from the start. Your children need you and you need your children.

You should be the "Wonder Woman". Be the "Super Mom", your children deserve it and they can benefit from it as well. What the schools fail to teach, you become the teacher and teach them when you can. Give them life's true lesson, so we in the future can all benefit from your strong being. You have the first chance over all to mold a good decent human being, and be as impartial as you can to allow lessons to be learned and not missed. Remember life is short and when your kids love you, your life is great.

Which mother are you?

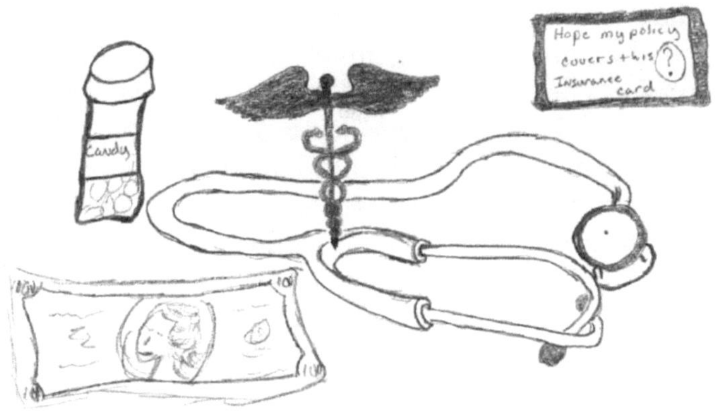

Let's think about it. You get sick and you need medical assistance. So you go to a doctor or you go to the hospital. You get there and you wait to get this help. Here is the interesting part: before you can even be seen you are asked the time old 20th century question: "Do you have your insurance card?" Well, if you look at the Hippocratic Oath, it's nothing in this oath that has anything to do with insurance because they helped and received donations for their work. That's another story; I want to talk about the system. We have not perfected space travel and our planet does not get bigger with age and we have grown double the size of the humans on the planet in only 100 years. The rich keep you in the dark and they force you to sign your life and spend years of your hard earned money, because you were given confidence that you put your money in and later you can take it out. Good plan isn't it?

No interest rate is added for simplicity. Let's say, you put 300 of any currency in these institutions for once a month for a 10 year period, that's 36000 - not much right? Now you have a company with 500 workers doing the same thing. Now that's 18,000,000; OK, now if you like, just add the interest rate over 10 years from each quarter. That's a lot of money; you should be covered when you walk into the hospital. So when you go there and the bill is 3000, why is it that you have to put up with all the hassle to begin the operation? There are plenty of technical engines you can draw from to answer my question, but this is just the smallest part of the issue.

Very powerful groups feel that most of you should not live, because you are wasting food and resources and they are running out of reasons to feed you. Look on the shelves and what do you see? They are full right? Look at the ingredients and you will see nutrients are little to none. They spend years on how they will tell you what the next illness will be, so they can justify the increase of your donation. The same substance that is used to kill rats is use to brush your teeth. Now they want to put it in the water to destroy brain cells and give you arthritis later in life. Yes, we are now stuck in a world of placebos and we call it "health care".

Well, your government does not care about it and they will always be reluctant to make it better. If this were the case, then why is it deteriorating by the day? They don't practice, what they preach; how can you have faith in a system called government, when they resist to do what's right? Why do veterans have to go through an overextended paper trail, just to get aspirin? Why seniors are the last on the list for health care? Why does a man have to rob a bank for one American dollar just to get health care? Funny, prisoners have better health care then the average man working and doing the right thing. Guess, we should all break the law; at least we will be healthy. Why do doctors have to reject health treatment due to they cannot accept your policy? I guess all money is not good money in their eyes, especially yours is not good as well.

Government in Latin or (GUBOR MENTE) means control the minds.

Funny isn't it? (We will see this word again.)

Really funny when you see this but put this in a true perspective. The best way to control mankind is through their mind. Some folks will call me an atheist, but I am not. The reason, why the fallen angels have the advantage is because we are all not on the same sheet of music. The three main religions of the world are the Jewish, the Christians and the Muslims. Now it is time to show the result of ignorance of mankind. Three religions: for centuries they have fought each other to be the better religion. Funny, but they all believe in the same god. Jews in the exodus committed genocide as they left Egypt; Christians had the Spanish inquisition where they committed religious genocide of suspected non-Christians. Ghazis for the faith of Islam initiated the conquest of the infidels; this was for them a religious duty. Ottomans started jihad and their belief was that non-Muslims should be subjugated by the sword.

Was it religion or was it monetary growth? Man has made religion a business and this is very dangerous. When you read their literature it promotes peace and harmony for all mankind, but it's not the case. Just because a person follows this concept, they are murdered or get chased out of most societies. Some regions live together in peace for years and only, because they acquire enough guns to overthrow the religions in their town who have an association to a different religion; they are executed or displaced. This is the result of loving God under man's conditions. It's funny that they all bleed the same, they can have babies, they have the same diseases, they eat the same foods and they hated each other so much, they forgot why. The leaders of these organizations live in luxury, while the followers scrape by to feed their families and pay their bills. Makes you want to really wonder: is this God really worth it? Some of them have taken such steps to solidify their level of "the one and only" that they claim, they were chosen distinctly by God, that they were the only race that he wanted out of all the others. Funny the same people treat another civilization like animals in a cage.

Another religion will not even let you draw their prophet and will protest in the streets. They claim they can't burn their holy book, yet these members have torn down their places of worship and yes burned their holy book - and not a word was said, but when someone outside this religion was told by Governments of the world that it was unethical to do what these people have done. They have to step back because it appears to hurt the worshipers of that books feelings. The next religion literally has killed people, only because the person did not believe in their way to practice this religion; it accused people of being witches and devil worshipers and death was the only way to salvage their soul.

If God is so powerful, why is it that its worshipers are so scared to answer the hard questions and live in fear? When they can't answer these questions, they just state you must have faith. Each one of these religions where published centuries after the events they claim happened. Their books have been edited for years and translated so much that I think the truth was lost.

I believe in God, but I refuse to let a man tell me how to worship my God. Man has made God a business, a murderer, a racist, a player of lives, a real estate agent and Hippocratic deity. I don't think God had this in mind, when he made men. Religion is manmade and it is full of holes. If it takes food out of your mouth or money out of your pocket, you might want to think, what you are dealing with. There were 12 disciples that followed Jesus why are there only 4 Gospels? Where are the other 8? Why are these books lost? What was the reason they were taken out or set aside when this book was published?

If you would follow your religion the way it is supposed to be followed the world would be a different place.

And you thought it had horns.

Yes, you knew this had to be the next subject. Satan, the devil - or whatever you decide to call this creature, he is the most intriguing of all. People love beautiful things, so why is this creature portrayed as a beast with horns and a tail, holding a pitch fork? Yeah, you see this and you will surely run, but think about it: if it were so ugly it would be easy to resist? It's not. When you read about the story of this creature, it was one of the most beautiful creatures, God has ever created. Among all of the angels, this creature was given a percentage of God's powers. They accuse this creature of being jealous of mankind, and this started a revolt that rocked the heavens. The creature lost this war and was cast out of God's presence. When you read more about this creature and when you read closely, you will find that it is not the reason for the so called "sins" you commit. This creature just sets the stage for you to fail. This image of this creature was created in the middle ages and the reason was, because the people in this region really did not take religion serious, because they had more interest in other things like providing for their families. The priests began a campaign on preaching about this creature and gave people, who really had not much intellect, something that would solidify this creature's existence. It has very little representation on the holy books and yet it is the most feared creature in the realm of religions. The best thing that Satan has done was convince the world that it does not exist. I believe Satan is the part of our inner self that we restrain from, because this creature sits and watches as we fight with in our minds what is right and what is wrong.

We have made this creature the scapegoat of all of our wrong doings and this seems to be a paradox, because we were blessed with free will to do as we please. This makes it even easier for the creature. It's like we convince ourselves that our commitments are either good or bad and this drives us to insanity. Man has created sin, not Satan. He just enjoys as you do what you perceive as sin and he knows that all you have to do is know God and you will be saved. It was said many times, how man knows what God is going to do when we die. What if all - and I mean all - of our actions was accepted and had little relevance to God? Would you feel you have lost your chance to explore yourself and what you could have done?

I believe Satan loves the fact that greedy religious leaders exploit it as the tool of control. Remember, in the

Christian book supposedly Satan or the snake asked Adam and Eve, why they don't go to the tree of Wisdom and Knowledge to learn more of God and the purpose of your existence. They had the opportunity to move on and live in the zoo or lab, God has provided for them. They went to the place where this knowledge was kept and "no I don't think it was not a tree." Together they pursued this knowledge and I sure would like to know, what they saw and why they were banned from the presence of God. Are you sure, we are on the right track? He, who wins the war, gets to tell HISTORY OR HIS STORY.

What if we were on the wrong track and he was trying to help us and from an eviler fate? It is funny, how beautiful things are the most deadly on the planet. If you eat flowers you will become ill. If you eat broccoli you will become healthy. Still think this creature is the ugly beast you were told when you were young? See it's that easy to drive men mad on a simple concept such as Satan.

If you do go mad then I think this creature has the best of you.

Do the Homework

This little piece of paper makes the world go around; it is funny how this paper makes you happy and sad at the same time. We work for it, we fight for it, and we even die for it. This is the governments of the world's way of giving us some worth. This paper lets people know that they will have food shelter and transportation as long as they have enough of it. People will take this paper over things that we need to survive. People will do anything for it, given the right situation; and people are so obsessed with it that it appears to give them a euphoric sense that everything will be ok, when it is within their reach. People trade their children for it, people trade the abuse of their bodies for it and people even feel that given the right amount of it, they will own others to do their bidding.

We are all caught in this trap because it keeps us un-united and as long as we feel, it has worth, and we will never see the insanity it creates. What will it be worth, when there are no more farms? What will it be worth, when the fresh water runs dry? What it will be worth, when your stores have noting on the shelves? Will it matter that you have it or will it matter that you live to see the next day? This representation of worth is the reason empires have crumbled and people were left to starve. The only reason you may not see this is because your belly is full and you have shelter to rest in and you can just jump into your mode of transportation and travel from one point to the next. People have traded their selves for labor with the ones, who have accrued enormous amounts of it. It forces you to forget the fundamentals for survival, making food from scratch use to be a way of life.

Now it is considered an art form. Planting a garden use to be for giving ourselves a surplus of food in the seasons the plant could not grow. Now it is just a hobby that most bored house wives or husbands do until their other half comes home. It was normal for people to know how to do repairs on their homes and now we pay professionals to plug a hole in our roofs. This is all, because we find worth in this paper that is made from recycled goods; we threw away in the past.

Do you think this is a stable source for a future? Well... No it's not at all; it is the world's transference of debt from one hand to the next like the game hot potato. Who ends up with it last loses. This paper is a loosely controlled credit scheme to give the lower classes security to accumulate items, they think they need. Money is no longer two chickens for one bag of flour. It is now a form of light and all you have to do is press a button and it appears out of nowhere, it took on a new form, so we cannot see it for what it is. This server based system is protected by the worlds governments to keep even more control on its citizens and preventing the possibly that it will lose worth and can be no longer be traded for goods. When the empire falls, what will you do then? You don't know how to plant, you don't know how to raise livestock and you don't know how to fix your mode of transportation. What will you do?

All of this happened before and it will all happen again. What will happen to you?

The color of skin is only the beginning.

The perfect race this is what they strive for and they took great measures to reach this point. They traveled to Tibet to find what was considered the advanced race from Atlantis. These super beings could be known as gods like Athena and Zeus, who were forced to flee their homeland because it sank in the sea. They made it to this region and did not find what they were looking for so they pushed on. They built an empire and they had a war machine which, if fueled properly, would change the world we know today. Well this did not work so well and they lost and went into the shadows, only to return in different sects.

To most of the followers they only knew the surface of this movement. Now they prey on the un-educated and poverty stricken to keep their cause alive.

Just remember skin is only the beginning. Once there are no more colors to choose from and the world is cleansed of the darker beings. There will be only one race to choose from and you guessed it: the one race which wanted a colorless society.

Now the fun begins; you will be put in cast according to your genes. Some of you will be the slave class, because your genes will have residue of the dark and weak races you have destroyed that are present within your genes. A new prejudice is formed, which will be judged by your DNA. Deep isn't it?

All of you will be placed in your cast and you will watch, as your brothers with the stronger DNA will be pampered and given prestigious positions where you will be forced to salute or bow to which ever they see fit to honor them. All of you, who just joined to be a part of something, will be the next specimens for the higher echelons of this system to use in experiments. You will accept this, because they will make you believe, it is for the benefit of the race. You will be used for all sorts of projects, you and your body parts will be stretched to its limits as the higher echelons strive for immortality and once your body is used up and they have no more use for you, due to you have nothing more to use for this cause, you will be incinerated or fed to the animals and your fellow brothers in this cast will be next.

They keep you on the lowest level and they teach you to hate. They let you do all of their dirty work so they do not have to bear the brunt of the blame. They never tell you, why you are doing what you do, so they feed you with hate paraphernalia and scriptures to keep you blind of the ultimate cause. This is the future of this idea and you are just a pawn in their chess game. They want you to be proud of your race; yes but it is funny, how they will not stand up and support you, because it's not good for business. All you have to feel inferior is the labels you give other races and you use weapons instead of books to win your wars. Just one hint: the closer you bring your race the greater chance you have to have intercourse with your sister or brother and your children come out a lesser species. Remember, the oldest human remains were found in Africa, India and other regions of darker species. It was proven by your scientists that this is the cradle of civilization. Who knows? The darker beings could be the reason you do hate, because they sent you outside the village, because you were different. They did not kill you because they had respect for life. All your life you wanted to prove your worth to this society and you continuously get rejected because you looked different. See how easy it is to think of such stupid theories? In the end we all bleed the same as well as other traits.

Give it up; you're fighting a lost cause.

We were not always this way. We just wanted to have a decent way of living and freedom to explore our thoughts and dreams, to be a better society. Well, the world had a different approach to our fate. Yes, we have all the good toys and this was the beginning of our doom. We are now considered the policemen of the world. With this title, we live on a double edge sword and we as Americans let this go on. Since you do not exercise the rights our fore fathers fought so hard to give us, we have become the main society to love and hate at the same time.

"We the people; by the people; for the people." What does that mean to you? Well, for most of you; you don't have a clue. You passively sit in your living rooms and you look at your giant flat screen TV's and you let the Hollywood propaganda team dumb you down to the point, you cannot even determine what is real and what is fake. The majority of you do not even care, because you feel it does not affect you. Most of you are more interested in a rich reality TV star which has minuscule problems hypnotize you; and you have to worry about how you are going to make ends meet. You simply do not care about your country; you are just riding the band wagon to destruction.

Look at the result of your passiveness. You let businesses leave the United States and move to third world countries; now most of you are unemployed. You made no attempt to become part of your government and you left it up to the people, who want to profit from this institution to run the show. Why it is that Congressmen, Governors and Senators have 100% pensions after a 4 year career and Soldiers who puts their lives on the line for this institution earn 50% or less. Civilians work for decades and in the end still cannot live on the money they thought they saved and are forced to work the remainder of your lives. Funny, the heads of the big banks don't pay taxes and you do.

You spend millions of dollars on universities, which teach you nothing. After you finish your so called studies, you are deeply embedded in debt which you will never be able to pay. Instead of working for your future and paying for your home, you spend the rest of your golden years paying for your children's four to six years of school.

This elite group saw you coming a mile away. Now, they have you where they want you. Ignorant of your laws, dumbed down to your society. They have given you a god, whom you do not understand and you make their jobs easier, because when the truth is told to you; you laugh in the face of the resource. They suckered you into Income tax and social security, which there is a good chance you will never see. Now you fight wars, you have no clue you are fighting for. You walk around like you are at the top of the food chain. You parade around like there is no other. All of these illusions have captivated you, and you are in a ruse, and you do not see what you have given up. You think you are the best in the world.

When all you are is the equivalent of the emperor with no clothes.

Fighting fire with fire really? What have you proved? Just like a child looking at the grown-ups and copying their ways. You thought guns and big parades were the way to freedom, well it just appeared to be useless. If you would have taken the time to meet in undisclosed locations, educated the masses and started your battles with the pen, instead of the modern day sword, you might have had a more profitable outcome. This is how the modern day wars are fought. The wars on TV are just a deadly masquerade. You should have restored the male cornerstone, which was obliterated during the times of slavery.

You should have created tight net communities that worked under the flood lines like the Israelis and Asians. You should have studied history and you will see how families such as Rothschild and Rockefeller managed to get results. They are the main players of today. It's sad that your so called enemy has given you the greatest access to knowledge you will ever see, and you are too lazy to learn, what they have to teach.

We have a legacy of criminals, teenaged pregnancy and passive over religious drones. Now you have rap music and R&B and you still screw it up. You have cultures all over the world wanting to resemble you and you don't teach them anything. You are still slaves, even today, all they did was: disconnect the leash. You are more associated with populating prisons, instead of universities. The ones with an education turn their backs on you, because you can't be controlled.

As for the educated ones you sold out. You are actors, musicians, doctors, teachers, bankers, lawyers and other professions; and you lock your selves in the same communities that your so called enemies build, to stay away from the products you create. You are still the little pet that gets to eat the scraps directly from their tables, while we - the alley cats - have to wait for the trash to come out. You have all your knowledge and you waste it for the sake of security.

You just don't get it, because you only see what's going on your block and not what is going on in the world. You have got to the point, where money is your driven path and you don't even know, how to make it. You fall into petty pickpocket schemes instead of making the real money. They give you drugs to sell and the sad part is you don't even own a cocoa or poppy seed field. You think this makes sense? They use you in sports and entertainment like jesters in a royal court. You help the madness of dumbing down the nation and you don't even see it.

Learn how to fight before you enter the ring. Make real differences, don't be a part of the madness. You can change the world you are letting slip between your fingers. Get into those communities, teach the ignorant, how to become smart and create a productive society. Break away from the common visions of thugs and idiots and become respected human beings.

Make a difference that counts.

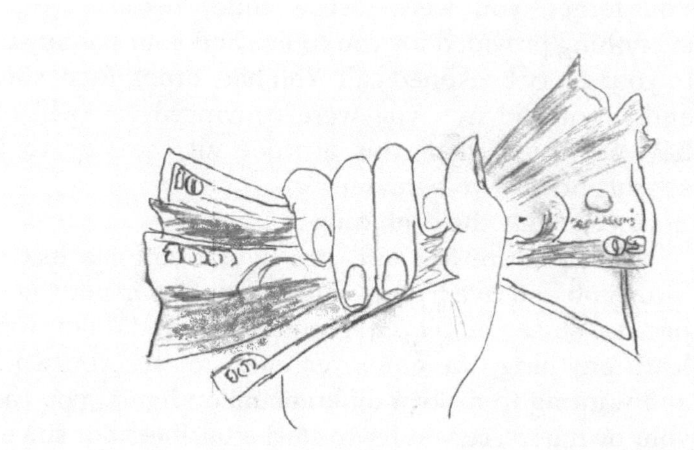

You wonder why your wallet or pocketbooks are just ornaments on your arm and back pocket. You work day in and day out and it seems like you just can't get ahead. You feel like there is no end to this madness; well just look in the mirror. You put yourself there - and you have not wakened up to realize it.

You were provided school - and you wanted to play. You were told that you will be given the secrets to success - and you were more worried about recess. You did not do your homework - and you watched TV or played with your toys. You did not read that chapter in that book, because the weekend was too precious to give it up for a few words. You did not raise your hand in school, because you did not care to be at the top of your class. You felt school was a waste of time - and you would not need it.

You forget, you were just a child, because you had everything provided for you to live and your parents came to your every beckoned call. You had a roof, food, shelter, and if you did not, you were convinced you will never have it. You carried this attitude all the way to high school and now you are free.

This is only the beginning...

Now you are free and you figure, you can just walk into a job and live happily ever after. This is not the case, because since you played around and you did not want to learn anything, the employer does not see you working and wanting to make a difference. You figure, you can be your own boss, so you try to start a business but since you did not learn advanced math and study law, you don't know where to start. So you; as you did all your life look for the easy way out, and this does not work.

You sit in your parents' house and they wonder when you will grow up.

Let's say you did study, you made the grades. You graduated, you get the dream job, but you did not bother to learn the reality from the text you were taught. You just regurgitated the information, but you never learned. You get the job, you think life is good, but you never learned true financial education. You stack up credit cards, you go to the banks for loans, you finance everything you have and you own nothing, because you did not pay off the cards and loans you made in the past, and you live beyond your means. You keep this cycle and one day you find that the money you spent, "you did not have" is wanted to be returned to the creditor you barrowed from. Since you did not pay off your debt you claim bankruptcy and you lose it all.

You find God, but what you did not encounter is that the God, you are worshiping, needs money to keep the lights on. Funny how your religious leader drives a fancy car and you walk to your building of worship on your holy day of worship. Funny your preacher eats steak and goes on religious retreats to luxury resorts and you eat beans and rice and have no chance to go on a retreat, because you can't afford it. Funny isn't it?

You don't have it, because you never learned, how to make it and make it work for you. You did not want it, because if you did want it; you would not be in the situations most of you are in today.

It's not too late; learn how to make it, so you know how to spend it.

Are we countries or are we corporations? Who are the real leaders? (GUBOR MENTE)

This is interesting, because you see the politicians as they sell you a great story and you depend on them to carry your thoughts and views to make your country a better place. You go to the voting booth, you choose your candidate, and you think you have made a difference. Well did you ever notice that what they told you and what they have done happens little to never? You get mad for about ten minutes, give up and you wait until the next election. Don't you feel like an idiot? I guess not, because you do it all the time and you never follow up on your concerns. You have been brought to the point that you do not even care, who is at the podium, because your voice will not be paid attention to.

"Stupid ass…" It's your government and you do have a say in it. It is OK though; a group of people have already made decisions on your life for you. Yes it's true, you have given a group, you do not even know, the power to run your life and tell you where and when you can go and what you can have and not have of your earnings. They are called corporations.

Do you really think the governments of today want you to have a better way of life? If you think so, then you are already a victim. They want you to stay in your fence and graze in the field, they let you roam free around, and you could face major penalties, if you break the fence and cross the street to eat better grass. They send you to wars, you have no clue about. They tell you that you are too skinny or too fat. They provide you with false images of how you are supposed to look. They poison you with experimental drugs that only prolong your sickness. They have convinced you that food with no nutritional value is the best way to enjoy yourself and be healthy. One decade, they tell you not to eat certain meats. The next they tell you to eat the same meat that they did not want you to eat in the past. Now they don't want you to eat meat at all. They tell you that you are the cause for carbon dioxide, but do not tell you that it was at higher levels eons, before you even existed. They do not want you to be healthy, because guess what? They have to feed you and if you are healthy, you will multiply and they will run out of food and shelter to give you. They tell you the value of your money and what is legal to spend on or trade.

The corporations spend millions to make this all possible. They find a candidate, who will work in their interest, flood their accounts with money, buy off the competition and get their candidate in the main offices of government to control you, keep you stupid and keep you under control. They provide you with luxuries like TV's, video games, sports events, automobiles, and Sex to keep you at bay. While they slowly bring you to a point that you cannot think for yourself and you lose a sense of reality what is really going on around you.

They put you in a state of euphoria, while they bend you over and rape your mind. It's not about race, it's not about money, it's all about control and power. You let them have this.

"It's just business... "

In the beginning, GOD was something man believed in for spiritual comfort, this GOD was an entity, which gave man direction and a sense of self-worth. This GOD could perform miracles, raise the dead and was infinite in its life span. This GOD taught us how to live our lives in harmony, how to rejoice in him, because he provided us with comfort, as long as we recognized him as our true deity. This indeed was a good time and it was something beautiful to have this GOD in our lives. This concept is the most confusing, because man uses this GOD to create another GOD. This new GOD is now the current GOD, but it is only for the wealthy and powerful man to believe in; though we, the common man, believe in the original GOD. We are controlled by the wealthy man's GOD and the sad part is we let it go on.

"The Father" (Gold) is powerful as well as beautiful. It gives us strength and it gives us a sense of fulfillment. We love it, we always want it around, and we feel complete, when we have it. It gives us all, we desire and with it, there is no other that could compare to its power and glory. Men will die for it; men will do all, they have to do, to possess it. Empires were raised and empires fell because of it. Men could control the masses with it. Just to wear it meant: you were something special and you should be respected. Mankind will sell their body and soul to have it in their lives. In some cases - with certain groups - it can give you a free ticket to meet the first GOD it represents and live happily ever after.

"The Son" (Oil) has many uses and is just as old as "The Father". It has always been there to light dark tunnels and allows us to see in the dark, it was the power of true light. We cook with it, we clean with it. "The Son" had multiple uses. In its evolvement, we transport goods with it. We transport ourselves with it; it can create tools, which we use to make our lives easier. It is not as beautiful as "The Father", but it has the same power as "The Father". With it we also can have the same gifts that "The Father" gives. Our live will seem empty without it and our lives will be empty without it.

"The Holy Spirit" (Drugs) - although this is the younger of the two - we still fall within its grasp. We know it is bad, we know it is wrong; but it feels so good, when we are in the presence of it. It enlightens us; it gives us a new outlook on life. It takes us to a whole new dimension and with it we can forget all of our problems as we feel forgiven for all the sins we have committed, when we indulged in it. The wealthy use this to control the masses as well. They pay governments to move it over borders. The wealthy gets "The Holy Spirit" on the streets and they give it to the poor to forget their problems and the rich whom they feel should not be rich, to be either incarcerated or die from their indulgence. Scary isn't it?

Who is your GOD? When you speak for GOD and country, what does it mean to you? Why are you letting the wealthy man's GOD control you?

What does one nation under GOD mean to you? "In GOD we trust".

It's an interesting concept, if you know who GOD is.

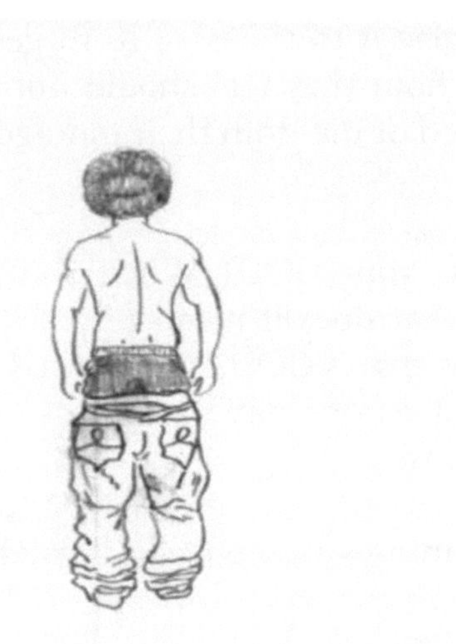

Yes you seen this guy, he is the at the height of fashion and when he walks down the street, the girls just follow him like a hungry Pit Bull Terrier chasing a steak. This gives him confidence and this makes him feel like a man. You first seen it in the Rap Culture and in some cases it's still there. So many so called "role models" (who claim not to be role models) still display this style. To the young crowd, this is the way to go, and if you add a sleeveless undershirt, tank top - also known as the "wife beater" - you can go into any establishment and get respect.

Do you really know where this style came from and where it originated? You read this and you are wondering now and this is why knowledge is important, when you are dealing with the Pop culture. Pop culture is the most obscure culture, you can ever deal with. The most interesting about this is that it transforms any symbol or fad or trend to appeal to the masses - and the generation it is embarking on has no clue. They just accept it, because their "role model" says it's "KOOL" in their own way. This phenomena captivates society's and it gets to the point that you end up with cookie cut entertainment groups, trying to win sales from three to four different beat mixes. This is why the young males and a few females wear their pants like the picture you see in this section.

This code started in the prison system, but be careful, because people also thought people in prison (inmates) needed to know who was straight and who has not been turned into a potential "Homo Thug" (Gay or Bisexual Prison Inmate). Well it was in this institution, because there were only generic sizes to give out and inmates did not have a choice. Only the inmates know the truth of this phenomenon and you would have to have been in prison to really know. So, when you are profiled by the law and you have no clue, why that law official looks at how you are dressed; this gives these officials a big hint. So, just think about it, when you get your "swag on", what you are telling the world, when you walk down the street? Do some research, it will surprise you how the prison has a society of its own as well. This so called code to the system, "To the ones who did not research it means": ready or available" to sexually please them in any way.

It is a shame that "real prisoners", who steal, rape, kill and sell drugs and stolen goods to their community, are selected to be role models, instead of real heroes (whom also are put in prison), who do what they can to better your life and sacrifice their freedom for you.

All you look like is a guy who can't afford a belt and if you could, you did not know how to wear it around your waist. Makes you think, when you see theses "thugs" walking down the street, who are supposed to be tough. Well, if you see them showing their underwear, I guess you have a clue of just how tough these thugs really are and what you can expect, when you are confronted by them.

I am not attacking the Homosexual society. To each of you your own that is the choice you made under free will. This is for the mindless Pop Culture Drones, who just imitate the corrupted role model and conduct no research of whom they follow.

So I say to you, who don't know the code, if you want to let the world know that you gave them permission to bend you over the table, and take your pants further down your waist to your ankles, wear the code of the penal system; let the dominant of this society give you the ride of your life. Show the world that you can take it up the ass and still smile when it's over.

For the rest: well have fun and if you did not know, then now you know. Learn the code, so you know who and what you represent.

Well this picture should speak for its self, and when you see it, you cringe. You sit at home and look at the celebrity reality shows and music videos and you see these women, who are half dressed or give the appearance that instead of a wardrobe, they own a paint shelf because they appear to have painted on their garments to walk down the street. You then go to the shopping center and you and your girlfriends conduct an all-out assault on the clothes racks or shopping spree; and you buy the tightest and most exposed clothes on the rack. You do this because you want to be at the height of fashion and you want to look good, when you go on your next girl's night out. You buy your selections and you walk out the store, ready to conquer the social scene. Nothing can stop you; no one can stand in your way. So why is it, when you finally put this selection on, and a man is walking toward you, looking at your selection with lust, do you adjust your clothes as if you are underdressed? You give him a glare, like he is not allowed to look at you and you have images of men being perverts; and you think how can they look at you in this way? Yeah you're not a slut or a whore or nympho; he has no right to look at you in this way.

Well guess what?

Don't wear it, if you don't want to feel this way. How can you think this way, when you set the stage for the event to occur? There are plenty of fashion pieces that can give you the attention you want without the "glare" and if you want a man to give you this respect, then dress for the occasion not for the pimp. You have convinced society that it is okay to dress like a whore and give you respect; but the interesting part of human nature is that men will be men on all levels. 40% of skin exposure tells a man that you are hot and sexy and you could be a potential keeper. This is the average cocktail dress. Less than 40% tells a man you just want to have friends with benefits or one night stands. More than 40% tells a man that you are not in the market and they will be better off, if they leave you alone. You can wear what you like but, just be ready for the affects you create, when you wear your fashion piece. It's not KOOL to be part of the cookie sheet and fit into the box like the others. This means: stand out in a positive manner, if you want a positive result. Did you ever wonder why some girls do get the good ones before you? Do you remember what you did to be with your man and why he loves you to death? It's because these women where honest with them self and these men - and you were honest with him. Take the time to establish a firm foundation, when you are out on the prowl or hunt. What you wear gives the potential mate an idea of what he is about to embark upon and dressing for the results you want is the key to your success. Dress as you like; but be ready for the results from your actions. If you dress like a whore, expect to be called upon as a whore. If you get this, just remember you did this to yourself and you cannot really put all the blame on the men, when they see you like this. You send out a message every time you walk out the door and you have to be aware of this. Silent signals are the most misunderstood, when it comes to human beings; so it reduces a lot of confusion when you know what you want and what you expect when you choose the fashions of society.

Think before you act, keep your dignity intact.

Every year you see all of these natural disasters and you have to ask: Why did this happen? As you sit and watch the TV; and you see these poor souls as they struggle to get to the nearest of safe haven. For the next few weeks the great campaign is on and you dig deep into your pockets, you send those folks tons of money; you feel you have done your part and now you can sleep at night knowing that you help these poor souls get through this terrible time.

Well wake up. Where does all of this money go? Do your research or just look at the TV, you are so in love with, and you will see that it just disappears and you never see it again. Africa is probably one of the richest and most fertile lands in the world. Yet the majority of people ever since the 20th century and maybe before still make only the equivalent of $2.00 a day. Funny isn't it? Haiti had an earthquake and billions of dollars where contributed to the cause - and still today it lives in poverty, where so called housing is replaced with tents from some military surplus. Roofs are covered with tarps with logos like UNICEF and other sales pitching devices. These people never see these monies at the lowest level. WOW, 11 billion dollars for 9 million people and nothing to show for it.

Germany asked the school children to bring in the Euros but never asked where it went. When you walked in the gas station, you seen a jar with a hand written sign labeled "For Haiti", and it was almost full before the end of the day.

Where did the money go? Governments see this as basically a "free for all collection" and you drones fall into this trap all the time. They spend the years telling you, how broke they are and that they cannot spend money on infrastructures and benefits you pay for.

It's funny how they can still take their private jets and drive through town with loads of SUV's and luxurious cars, stepping out and waving at you on the way into that big mention or that 5 or 7 star hotel, smiling because in their minds they are laughing at you and thinking "look at all of these idiots".

You dump tons of money into this institution and you still struggle to make ends meet. Then, when you need this benefit, they make it such a hassle to get them, and they hope you just give up. So when the flood wall breaks and now you own nothing, just think of your contribution to these agencies. Just think of when you drive down the street and you hit a pot hole and get a flat.

Where did the money go? Not enough money; makes you wonder. Common sense could fix this but it does not exist in modern government or any government since man created it. They get away with it, because you let them. If you know that your house is not sound for your environment, then why do you build it? If your Levy is falling apart, then why don't you make the repairs to fix it? All our knowledge of irrigation and you just sit there and watch you lives float away. You do this, because you have been trained to be babysat by these organizations and you don't even see it. You drive and walk by millions of problems in your neighborhood and you continue to think it is bigger than you. Then when the emergency hits, you run for the government to save the day. They spend millions of dollars and the problem never gets fixed.

Self-educate your communities because the government will not. You have so much skills and talent being lost every day, and it's sad your towns and you don't even begin to rebuild your community. Picking up the trash in the street is a great start; because it leads to bigger projects like community infrastructure.

The real leaders are gone; now they are just business men who love to steal your money.

It's your government and you lose it every day you look the other way.

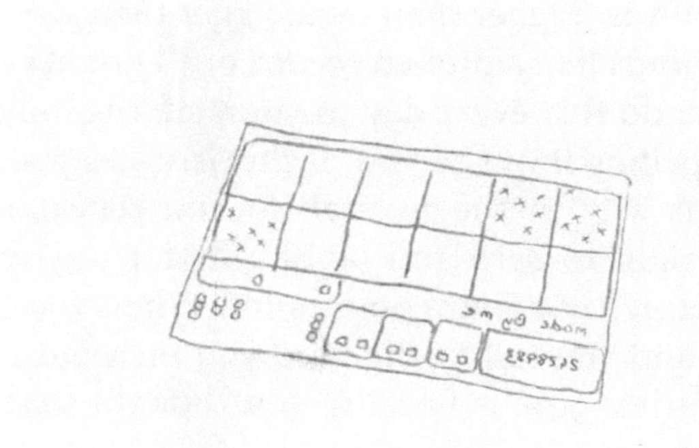

Make your own lottery ticket. Why not?

The modern world is a big place but, this 2 dimensional thinking which is a sickness of the 21st century, is what we are regressing to every day. Society constantly tells us that we just can't have the finer things in life.

Why do you believe this? Who has the right to tell you that you need to sit in your cubical and shut up? It's all over and all around you and you just sit there and once again you think: "this is bigger than me". Through your life you get sucked into negative peer pressure, you accept the opinions plus the so called criticism and you internally downgrade yourself to a class you can cope with.

Why can't you have the big car, the big house, the nice yacht in the sea? This is because of you having giving up on your hopes and dreams. As long as you let someone tell you what to do and how to do it, it is you putting yourself in danger of living a life you hate. You continue to think that it is "bigger than me...bigger than me...bigger than me. Sounds like a broken record or CD right?

Well you do this every day to yourself, the only crime I did was: spelling it out to you. If this irritates you in this format, then why in the mental do you repeat it? You have every right to earn and build a better way for your life, your family, and your community. When you give up your rights and you follow the herd you miss out on a lot of opportunities: 90% is because you thought that this is bigger than you.

What if billionaires thought this way? Well I would not have been able to write this book and write it with ease. These individuals are worth more money than most people could count. Why is it they get to do what they want when they want and how they want? This is because they believed and had a dream. Stop grazing the fields and become of the herders and not the cattle. Jump the fence and get some of that good grass across the street (not drug related). If they can eat it so can you. Why can't you be "too big to fail" just like the banks around the world.

Think about it: if you can't pay your bills; isn't it nice to know that your government can bail you out with its citizen's money and not yours? You can make fake deals and the people don't even get mad at you because they all think that it is too big for them to try. They do this to you every day; and they get to sleep with full bellies whiles you fix rock soup for the kids so they fall asleep. Yes rock soup, you have not heard of this delicacy? It is found in most third world countries. This is the process where the mother has no food to feed the kids. They only have one room or a tent to live in and the children have no choice, but to be in the same room where the mother prepares their food. She lays them down puts the cover over them and tells them to wait or sings until the delicacy is finished. She takes some big rocks and puts them in a pot makes a fire adds water and the child just stares at the pot and the mother stirs the delicacy until the child falls asleep. Tasty don't you think? Think about if you create a business on the internet and you charge 1 dollar to review and/or buy the products available, think in what could be referred to as 4th dimensional thinking. Social sites have over a million and more, what if half of them spent that dollar? Well you just made your own lottery ticket. This is just one way of looking at this.

Unfortunately we have lost this as we left the 20th century and if we don't see what we are doing to our self we all can enjoy some good old rock soup. It's not too big for you. You just need to know how to climb the steps of life and not the steps to your bedroom. Revitalize your dreams and hopes this is all we have and this is what makes us so great over the species around us. Be more than a consumer it's your right and you deserve to make your own lottery ticket. You can have an idea that can be worth billions too. You just have to step forward and pursue the happiness you deserve. It's not bigger then you. It is your problem to solve. You have to fix the madness this world has created. It is up to you if we see the 22nd century or not. Yes the world depends on you to do your part to give us a better future. If this sounds funny or stupid to you then you have not realized how away from your dreams you diverted from.

It all starts with a dream. It starts with you...

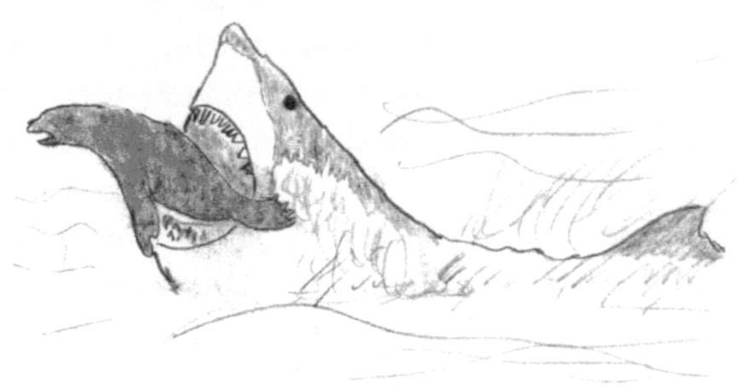

For those of you who do not know what these people, here is an example, a loan shark is a person or group who gives you loans under any circumstance and you sign a contract to pay it back. You get the money and you use this money and you put yourself in a comfort zone for a short period. Then comes PAY DAY and you can't pay it back the same way you got it. They make you think they are humble and forgiving but beware; the phrase "it cost me an arm and a leg" comes into whole a new light when they come to collect. If they were nice they give your stomach a good work out with their fist or a baseball bat. Second time they may break an arm, third time you become their slave and you are forced to do things you would not want to do. Every time you encounter this group they raise the cost to pay it back. Although the banks currently by law cannot take these measures, they get you in another way. Its call interest and it can be just as painful.

The banks are even more sinister then a loan shark because they give you a loan and they add this interest. They first reel you in and basically wave the cash in your face and hypnotize you with the numbers; once they take you through a long drawn process they go to the back to the manager's office where they sit back and laugh at how they are going to profit off of your stupidity; as you make little to no effort to bring cash to go against this loan to lower the monthly payments. They know you need the money. This is why they want to know your bill history, so they can know just how much they can take from you, so you live on little to nothing on your earnings. They really do not care that you have a good credit history or not, because they know that just to get you in the office took a lot, because you have done all you could do to meet your financial goal and could not meet them. Once they get you in this trap, they start you off with a payment you can afford. Then as the quarters come they conveniently let you know they are going to raise this interest and the game has begun. Yes there are some of you whom had it good and you manage to meet this goal but this number is small compared to their agenda. So by the time you come to the end of your payments you will have paid a high percentage of what the original amount was. If you cannot meet this goal remember there is no refund and you lose it all.

This is funny in its own way because the majority of people feel that it is possible because the paper work is so confusing, and you sign so many documents you forget what you have signed almost. They don't want you to read the fine print, that's why they created fine print and if you brought a magnifying glass to the table they would turn you away. This is because we are too lazy to read it and too desperate to think twice of what we are doing. Your payment will rise and you will pay more at the end. Yes remember your interest rate goes up so the monthly rate goes from 600 in currency now becomes 800 in currencies. You know you cannot pay this. Well they knew this would happen too; it's called refinance, think you are out of the hole not necessarily remember you just turned a 30 year loan into a 40 to 50 year loan in the end. They also found a way to rob you as well. They call them bundles. This is when a bank takes your mortgages and put them together selling them to a bigger bank that puts your mortgages on the global market. This is neat, right? They are depending on you to fail so the investors can profit. You will think that you are safe in your home and 15 years after you were into your investment and as soon as the bank goes belly up so does your investment. You did all the right things and you still loose. Sounds like a bad story right? It gets "better". You put your money in these banks and they tell you they will give you 2% on their earnings from your money. Well... what happens to the other 98% its profits off of your money? You open a savings account at the bank. The bank pays you interest on the money that you deposit and leave in that account. The bank then loans that money out to other people, only they charge a "slightly" higher interest rate on the loan than what they pay you for your account. That's how they make money.

Know what you are doing before you get fed to the sharks.

Just because it looks pretty on the outside does not mean it will look pretty on the inside. I am not referring to the house; I am talking about the scam. You need to know what you are getting into before you sign your life away.

TAKE YOUR TIME AND READ THE DOUCUMENT! It's your money and no one can tell you how to spend it. Yes it really is your money even if they gave you the money for it; why should you do what they want you to do just because they think it is best for you? They don't know you; you are just another profit they can milk off of and they could care less after you have signed the contract. Just remember you are about to invest a lot of time and money in your new home so you should spend the same time reviewing the documents.

If you are not sure go get some good advice from another source; it's your GOD given right to do this because it's your money. If a company or person asks for a fee in advance to work with your lender to modify, refinance or reinstate your mortgage. They may pocket your money and do little or nothing to help you save your home from foreclosure.

If they tell you they guarantee they can stop a foreclosure or get your loan modified. "HELLO!!!!" Nobody can make this guarantee to stop foreclosure or modify your loan. Legitimate, trustworthy HUD-approved counseling agencies will only promise they will try their very best to help you. Use your head and do the homework. If they advise you to stop paying your mortgage company and pay them instead. Despite what they will tell you, you should never send a mortgage payment to anyone other than your mortgage lender. The minute you have trouble making your monthly payment, contact your mortgage lender; be smart. If they put any pressure on you to sign over the deed to your home or sign any paperwork that you haven't had a chance to read, and you don't fully understand.

A legitimate housing counselor would never pressure you to sign a document before you had a chance to read and understand it. If they claim to offer, "government-approved" or "official government" loan modifications, they may be scam artists posing as legitimate organizations approved by, or affiliated with, the government. Contact your mortgage lender first. Your lender can tell you whether you qualify for any government programs to prevent foreclosure.

Remember, you do not have to pay to benefit from government-backed loan modification programs. Your government can help you if you know how it works. Also if you don't know the agent or business; and they ask you to release personal financial information online or over the phone. You should only give this type of information to companies that you know and trust, like your mortgage lender or a HUD-approved counseling agency. It will save you a lot of headache.

This is why a high percentage of you are out in the cold today because you did not know the "American dream" was achieved through hard work and paying attention to your actions. I am not perfect and I learned the hard way on many occasions; but the one thing I learned real fast was never to do it again. Learn off of others mistakes; they always tell you how they screwed up just don't be the one telling the story. Knowledge is the key this is not just some "KOOL" appliance from the shopping center, this is your house. Buy living above your means and looking for the easy way out you give these companies and people the chance to rob you blind. Taking that magnifying glass out, spending that extra day understanding knowing what you are about to do will save you from a disaster years later when you are well into your mortgage. Funny all you had to do is read and you would not have been in the dilemma you are in today. If you don't know the word bring a dictionary or make an "Ap" on your smart phone, this will normally discourage or even stop them in their tracks to try to go further with the scam.

Think about it; protect your homes, it is worth it to yourself and your family to do so.

This will be your future if you just live passively through life looking for the easy way out. A lot of you are almost there. Self-esteem and confidence is the most powerful weapon against this and it starts inside you. As long as you are healthy and can get out of bed, you should live your life to the fullest. Just because you are broke it does not mean you have to give up on your dreams. Education does not always come from a book. This is what the world appears to think education is. Education starts with an idea, problem, or a benefit. Look around you: everything and everyone can be used as a tool for you to grow and be successful.

You have experience, you have knowledge, and you have a brain. Why do you sit there and wait for your ship to come in when you live in the middle of the desert? Not much water there is it? So how will you get the ship to come in? Well you could walk to the water, that's one way; but you own this part of the desert so you don't want to leave. Why don't you build a road to the water and on the way build a canal to the water. Once you get to the water create a dam that you can turn off and turn on to regulate the water. Once this is done you then open the dam and let the water come back to your land plus since you found some folks on the way and they wanted to be a part of this project. You let them profit from all of the ships that use it and you convince them that you own 51% because you thought of it in the first place. They agree and you not only got the ship to your land the ship has to pay you to get there.

Yes this is just a fairytale but examine the steps that were taken to get there. This was because the person in the story wanted the ships to come to them and have and the water to take care of their needs. Why do you think there are rich and there are poor? This is because the rich keep as many people ignorant and needy as they can, to create an atmosphere for the ignorant and needy to rely on. They convince you that they are your only way out of the situations they create. Think of wars; normal people do not want to fight them. Rich people start them and the poor and needy are convinced that they have to support. Kings are Kings, Queens are Queens, and Presidents are Presidents; they are these figures, because you the common person let them think they are above you. If you ask the Royal Anal Cleaner how does the kings human waste or POO-POO smells, I GUARANTEE they will tell you that it stinks. You then ask why they do it. It's not because the king is handicap in any way. It's because it's the "KING" and no answer will be better. This person convinced the world they live in, that they are too good to wipe their ass and that someone below them needs to have this job.

Well not much has change because even today we fight for no reason; we steal for no reason, because someone who is rich drove us to do it in one way or another. We all sit in our cubicles and we live substandard lives and we are robbed of freedoms such as just being human. They taught the common person to do their bidding while they sit on top of the hill laughing as you walk into the sunset to do it. You have a right to live just as they do; but it all starts with you and how you take the steps to build self-esteem and confidence. This is what they did because they wanted the life they have more then you. They tell you not to steal, but they charge you interest on loans, they tell you that you are stupid, as they send their children to real schools. They tell you that you need to work, because you are too stupid to run and own a company. They make it complicated for the common person to maintain control, so they can continue to live the easier life. Rich people are lazy because you made them this way. They convinced you that you are so low; you end up like this picture and hate all the ones around you because you are this way.

As long as you let it go on and let your self-esteem and confidence diminish; you will be the person in the picture.

This is what cops may look like one day. Who is provoking whom?

Yes society has made the trusty police officer this way in the 21st century. This is the result because of lack of education in society and a few bad cops in between. From a criminals point of view it will be different. They surely deserve what they get. I say this because we have degraded our society to the point that our laws have become our enemies. Is this the price of real freedom? How can you call this freedom in this world when our enforcers of the law have to wake up every day of their lives praying that they can come home to their families? They used to be on your side. You turned your back on them every time you riot and break laws. The sad part is that it only takes one bad cop to screw it up for the rest of them. You as citizens set the stage for these people to become the images you see in this picture. Rioting in the streets, destroying property is stupid. The reason is because your taxes have to be paid to fix what you destroy when you go on your rampage. You take all this time and negative energy to make your point and you get mad when you get sprayed with the water cannon.

I will let you in on a secret. It takes 500 signatures in America to start the process for a law. If you took the numbers you rallied up 500 people to get 500 of these signatures peacefully; then you back a representative and get this individual on a ballot for your local election. You can make the law you that you wasted time fighting in the street for actually become your governments priority to do what you want and give these officers a rest.

In Germany, Member of Parliament refers to the elected members of the federal Bundestag Parliament at the Reichstag building in Berlin. In German a member is called Mitglied des Bundestages (Member of the Federal Republic) or officially Mitglied des Deutschen Bundestages (Member of the German Federal Republic), abbreviated MdB. The 16 federal States of Germany (Länder) are represented by the Bundesrat, whose members are representatives of the respective Länder governments and not directly elected by the people. In accordance with article 38 of the Basic Law for the Federal Republic of Germany, this is the German constitution; members of the German Bundestag shall be elected in general, direct, free, equal, and secret elections. "Interesting" you think? "They shall be representatives of the whole people, not bound by orders or instructions, and responsible only to their conscience".

This means you and your needs are to be represented by someone you put in office and the representative has to comply with your issues. These are just examples. Funny in some shape or form it's the people who have the final say whether you are a monarch or not.

So guest what? You can make the laws to fix your society and you are more worried about putting these people in a bad light. They attack you in such a way is because you living passively in your spaces moaning and wining about how society treats you so wrong. You make the laws, so you get what you get. If you took the time to study how your government functions, do you really think you will be suffering today? If you supported the police when they need your help you contribute to making a better society. You can make laws to create jobs so you don't have to steal. You can make drugs legal and tax it. The Netherlands did.

I'm not promoting drug use but back in the 20's in the United States liquor and other sprits was illegal and look at the United States now. "Drunk Drivers" are the leading cause for deaths in the country. We lose more people from drunks then we do in Iraq or Afghanistan.

Learn how to use your government so it works for you; and you can let these people enjoy the same privileges as you do. Stop going out there and being a hero by the sword, start with the mind. If they all believe in your dreams so will the police who shoot you with water cannons, and the law can take the real criminals of humanity out of society and restore the peace you deserve.

You have the power. You just have to know how to use it.

Why do you need so much? Why do you need it at all? These pictures were posted on these women's own free will. The fact is that the friends of these women were not being honest to them; and women not being honest to them self was the result of these masterpieces of cosmetology. Yes they look funny and yes they surely regret what they posted or whom they let post this image for them, now they have to go down in history as some of the funniest make-up fails. This is the extreme of what I am writing about but this is a message to all weather you put it on well or not.

Well just to let you in on a secret and its one that no one has ever been honest with you about. All of you are beautiful; the problem is that society stole the most beautiful possession away from you. That is, your confidence in yourself. You let society judge you, and wearing make-up is not the answer to beauty and you do not need it. You wear it to cover blemishes and acme you are too lazy to care for your skin properly and you do more harm than help when you cover it up.

If a man really loves or wants you, he will wake up to you more than once because you surely had to wipe it off to go to sleep. Truthfully we don't care about make-up; we care about the product behind the mask. If most of us could have it our way we would throw your make-up kit in the trash. The only men, who care about make-up, are the men who are more insecure then you.

Healthy bodies, women who are not afraid of a plate of food, women whom we can determine all of her body parts from a distance, women who know what they want and who they want; and yes men love obese women as well. Most men don't like skeletons. This means when you can see the bones and you can be used for a reference model for an anorexic clinic. Make-up can't hide those features, healthy and strong "real women" are what we want and these are the women who win in the end. Have you ever looked to see what is in make-up? Do you really know what you are putting on your face? Look up these chemicals if you like. Formaldehyde, Dibutyl phthalate, Dyes such as Benzyl Violet 4B (aka Violet 2),

Stearalkonium hectorite, Methylparaben, Salicylic acid, Glycolic acid, Coal tar, Lanolin, Sunscreens like PABA, cinnamates, mexenone, oxybenzone, Lead, Bacteria, some of you cannot even say these chemicals. In short, there are a lot of substances in make-up that can cause irritation to sensitive skin. This irritation leads to inflammation, which makes skin prone to infection and scarring. Furthermore, a nontrivial number of ingredients in cosmetics might give you cancer in the long run.

Believe me that cannot be pretty. If you're too lazy to look them up; just go on and keep putting it on your face and see for yourself. There are over 20000 ingredients in 80% of the products in today's market which are known to have caused adverse reactions in human as well as animal testing. Does that sound safe to you?

You might think that it does not make much of a difference. Think about this; these chemicals have been known to raise the risk of such serious issues as hormonal imbalance and birth defects and a whole lot more. Are you sure this does not matter? Why don't they tell us these things even though they must obviously know? If you don't know; then let me try making this a little easier for you to understand. Here's what corporations tell you; "what you want to hear" and what corporations don't tell you "what corporations know you don't really give a crap about". As long as you like the product once you have bought it, you will keep using it regardless of what you find out about it later.

Stop being selfish by covering all of that beauty behind a mask; men love to feel soft skin and not need a handkerchief in the end. Stop living like a cookie on a cookie sheet, steak taste good with or without barbecue sauce. You are truly the treasures of the earth and without you; we would not exist. Stop trying to paint over the masterpieces nature has given you.

If you can't resist then you consider slowing down before you regret what you have done in the end.

All of these years of suppression, all of the mistreatment and belittling and you don't want to finish what you started. This is not for the active ones who go day to day pushing for equality. I am talking about the women who want equality with "benefits". This is when you want all of the comforts of shivery and still assume you can get equality when it works in your favor, this is not right. It's all or nothing when it comes to equality and there is no middle. You wanted to be out in the work force you wanted independence but you let the real fighters do all of the work. Get off the band wagon and fight the good fight.

Stop being hypocrites: you are either for women equality or you're not. The real women don't need the dead weight. You deserve equal pay, equal health care, so help the ones who are out there getting these benefits for you. There are ups with equality and there are downs, you can't have the best parts of this system unless you work for it. Don't spend your time picking and choosing which part of equality you want. This is a pain in the butt for men when they depend on you to hold your weight when it counts. You are the reason why your sisters in arms have to struggle for simple benefits reserved still only for men. You sit in your corners and you watch your sisters in the streets in front of public buildings trying to get the male dominated society to give some breaks to you and let you enjoy a better life. You would rather be on your knees submitting to greedy and selfish men who just want you to open your legs, bend over "prepare yourself", keep your mouth shut, stay in the house, cover yourself in public, cook food and do what they say when they say because you are less than them. Society has taught our males that this is your purpose. It's sad that some groups of male dominated societies still think women are lesser beings. The Ancients considered that women were the same as gods. Where do you think the term "Mother Earth" came from?

You sit here and you put men in a situation that becomes confusing because you argue how you have a right to have the same jobs and privileges as them and when he puts you to the test, you cower and revert to phrases like "I am a women I can't do that". This is why a man can never take you serious. Some of you go the extra mile and it's obvious you simply cannot perform the task. I commend you but sweetie, if you can't do it don't get mad when he offers to help. The job must get done and time is money in this world today.

The subject of Adam and Eve is the most controversial subject in the world today. People have been strayed so far from the concept that they forgot the details of this story. Men always say it is your fault (the woman) why we are in this earth and why we live in such strife today. What men always forget is that they had the chance to say "no" to taking from the "fruit" of good and evil. Eve had a conversation with the serpent and was convinced that it was something to explore. She discussed this with Adam and at this time he could have stopped and do as God said and live happily ever after. He decided to agree with Eve and they indulged in the "tree of good and evil" and God discovered that they did what God did not want them to do. They were sent away from paradise and were cursed to live in this world we know as earth today. Man holds a grudge; because since then man mentally locks you in a cage for eons and you were forced to obey him because of this one sin of God. Guess what? It takes two to Tango, Adam made a choice, and what they fail to tell you: God did not punish Eve he punished Adam; Eve had no choice but to follow.

This is why we are living in this world today. He chose love over law. Now he feels that because of team work he was cast out of paradise. If he would have been a true leader we would have this paradise today. He fails you and he failed the world. We are in this together so we should all be equal. One over the other has failed, equality is the key. Adam should have been there to give Eve the strength to walk away.

Team work is the key.

When you see this I hope it strikes a nerve. Guys this is why the world is in such a way. We fear the concept of having children. This is the fault of society. Some of us hang in there till the end. For you who have given up; well your children grow up confused and they wonder where you went. Do you tell yourself it's too much pressure? It's too much for you to bear? It's her fault she needs to deal with "it". You may have a million reasons to give why you should not be in your child's life. Guys; be the better man. Women just don't wake up pregnant, or you can throw the Judeo-Christian concept out of the window.

You and her made these individuals and you leave the burden on her because you feel you have the option to run. Well you don't and you should take your responsibility.

You don't have to be rich; you just have to be there. Yes we make mistakes but society has given you a way out and this is wrong. We are not perfect.

Guess what?

Your child does not care. They just want know you exist. Children need a mother and a father. This makes us as humans complete. Fathers are the strength of the family and they are the part of the family that gives logic to decisions which keep the family strong.

Just look at the result of a fatherless family. Boys grow up feeling they can abandon all of their responsibilities. They have no respect for women and feel that they should not be taken seriously. Later in life they begin to hate women and become dysfunctional in relationships. Girls feel that all men do is run away from their problems and they have a low-self-esteem. They spend the rest of their lives hating all men making stronger men their father figures. This is not always good because what if their mentor was a pimp. By you being there you can put a curve in this process. By being the better man you can break the chain of this mad cycle.

How would you feel if your child became famous and you were not a part of this? Do yourself a favor; be there; because it's embarrassing when all of the fathers who stuck by there their kids profit from decent citizens they created; and you sit in the shadows as your child makes the speech of how they thank a man whom you do not know that gets all of the glory from your genes.

What if your child cured a deadly disease like cancer and your life was saved because of your child's effort? It would be really hard to say thank you, wouldn't it? These are just some of the accomplishments that you lose out on. I take my hat off to all women who endure the task of raising a child alone; even more if you survived abusive relationships to see that your child through.

Abusive fathers are just as bad as vacant fathers. You are weak and cowardly and you are a discredit to all society. You are the seed of most of the sexual pedophiles and criminals that exist today. You are too weak minded to realize what treasures you destroy. Abusive and vacant fathers are a great contribution to most of the criminals we deal with today. Great percentages of prisoners are the product of having no fathers to keep them in the right path. You can prevent this by just being there and being the better man. By you being there you contribute to great people. You can be many miles away and still be a good father. All your child has to know is how you have their back and they can count on you even if you make a few bad choices on the way. You are the rock of the world and you act like jelly and you have no capability to support your home.

GO HOME THEY NEED YOU!!!! GO BEFORE IT IS TOO LATE!!!! BE THE BIGGER MAN!!!!

NOW AS FOR THE QUESTION IN THIS SECTION. "It's not hard son because all you have to do is love. That is why I am here for you and you never have to ask this question again."

(All you have to do is love)

Why you have no clue what they are taking about.

There is a reason why they make the stock market so confusing. They don't want you to be rich. Every day when you look at the news (that's if you look at news) you see the screen full of numbers; and you always sit there and you just passively look at these numbers and they mean nothing to you. The digital ticker tapes as it streams; you see thousands of abbreviations with numbers. Did you ever wonder what they are? Well if you don't; it's just one more reason why you are broke and you are living from paycheck to paycheck. This is the best kept secret that the rich keep from those of you whom live in the nightmare you have created. This is another way the rich laugh in your face. There are millions to be made and you just sit there and let all of that money pass you by. If you understood this process I am sure you would not be in the situations you are today because it's so easy when you monitor the market.

Companies invite you to buy a share of their company and as they make money they pay you money for investing in them. If you do not understand what I just said; well this is the mockery that the rich flaunt in your face.

Schools don't teach you how money works in the modern world. Yeah there the universities but by then it's too late; because you are too scared to take the challenge they put before you. If such terms like Blue chip, Bear, Bull, Dow Jones, industrial average, P/E Ratio, Spread, NASDAQ and Book Value mean nothing to you; well you are way behind. This system is better than the lottery because you can almost predict when your fortune can grow. They kept you in the dark long enough to steal your house, reduce your 41k and charge you enormous interest rates on your credit cards. You all just feel that there is nothing you can do or you still linger in disbelief. The rich through a rumor can crush economies within seconds. There is no more real money out there but it's funny how the trading goes on. If you are wondering what they are trading with: well it's simple: "Nothing at all just debt that's it." "Really, they trade with nothing at all just debt."

Your money is just a piece of paper that your government tells the world that you can buy goods with. America laughs at you harder because they tell you directly on its currency that it is worth nothing. The phrase "legal tender" really means that your country will cover you even though this is not anything stable for trade. Our money use to be backed by the gold standard, this meant that for each dollar you had in your pocket was back by the equivalent of gold or silver. Once this was taken away by the Nixon cabinet we were doomed. Currency is the bottom if this chain, bonds and T-bills are the advance version. This is where the big boys play. Now you suffer from a weak dollar that can barely buy things you bought with ease in the past.

The rich bought off governments of the world and they in turn took near to all of the process of managing money out of the school house. They only teach you how to get a bank account, credit card and a checking account so they can play with your hard earned dollars on this market you know nothing about. This is the reason why most of you are unemployed; why you did not get that annual raise, why your unions are in the streets trying to get your benefits back. This is also the reason you get low interest rate earnings on your savings. These corporations together with the banks; work together to create a system that is so confusing that you as the pawn in this chess game are on a financial suicide mission which you may not recover once you try to jump in. They are dumbing you down and slowly making the food bank the new social center for survival. They wiped this concept out of existence as far as you are concern you are just happy being broke because being broke is easy. Wake up your intelligence and learn true financial management.

There is a gold mind streaming by you at the top of every news hour; learn how to use your economy and make it work for you.

Do you believe knowledge came from a tree?

Religion is manmade and man claims he gets his words from God. This is the theory the scientist and religious leaders spend the remainder of their lives trying to prove each other wrong. It appears that all of our Gods came from the sky and as crazy as it seems we still are lost. One thing that holds firm is man has dealt with beings from beyond this world. When you study the structures around the world and what you could come up with could be chilling. What if we were engineered from a society well advanced and we were put here to do its bidding. According some of the most popular religions mankind was created by the hand of this non earth being. As much as most of these western religions do not want to admit it is written that Eve was genetically created from Adam.

Today we have a much more vast knowledge of the stars and the mysteries of the world. Do you really feel that the knowledge of good and evil came from a tree? This is hard to believe because up until present there has not been a fruit or vegetable that we have eaten that would give us knowledge. Could this knowledge have come from an ancient computer data base or was it a book on a table? You have to think about what we as humans perceive as gods. Man passes information to the best of their knowledge of that day.

Take for instance back in the 40's when the Americans were occupying most Pacific islands. They came in planes and landed and these individuals never seen these machines in their lives. Later they left and the natives went back to their normal lives. They missed the rewards of food and other goods and they wanted to have these treasures again so they built model airplanes; hoping for the return of these considered gods. Imagine what their "bible" would look like if they were not rediscovered to be part of the 20th century. Why was this knowledge covered up by mankind over the centuries? Could it be that Adam and Eve knew something that they did not want to share and though time the secret passed through the eons that we to this day are not ready to know? Or did they pass this secret and man used this secret to wield power over the masses. What makes the story of Jesus so hard for men to fully embrace is that there are cultures older then this religion and they looked to the skies in a different light. Ancient culture what we know; recorded what they saw because they did not have the luxuries we have today for entertainment. What if we found out that these rewards which we are supposed to receive never existed?

In theory this would destroy mankind as we know it today. What if we found out that we were just a slave built for our so called gods' labor? When you look on the walls of ancient cultures they show evidence of what could be genetic engineering. Religion is man's way of controlling the masses as man started to implement their religions they became twisted. Europe took all of their people's literature and anything that could be perceived as knowledge giving; and for hundreds of years and generations they erased all intellect from their inhabitants. They then started to teach these people their way they and how they wanted them to live. This was easy because the people had no external sources to go off of except what was in the region. Why was this done? It's done because the ones who know this secret do not want you to know this secret because if you did they could not have any control over you. The funny part of it all is that now you are so lost and intertwined into lies and misleading practices that they put the secrets in front of you and you are too lazy to do the research and know just what exactly is on your planet and why it is here. All kinds of evidence lies with in ancient writings and structures that industries like Hollywood cause you to believe that these occurrences are just figments of our ancient's imagination. What if when Adam and Eve found out they were in a zoo or a lab? Have you ever looked at these places? The beautiful trees and when possible all the animals are in no less than two. They never have to worry about food, shelter. They do not need knowledge because all was provided for them. What if you woke up in the afterlife behind a cage? If you look into the history of your religion it might scare you.

Are you willing to take the chance and see what is beyond your nose?

Marriage symbolizes the union of man and women to make vowels to spend the rest of their natural lives together in harmony. This union has evolved over the centuries and it always been the symbol of love in the union of two souls. Man has also found a way to manipulate this as well. It seems as if it became more of a business contract then what it was to really represent. Man has made it easier to walk away from this union for the sake of convenience. Society has convinced most of mankind to not look at love as strongly as they should.

Marriage evolved into a business action this was for the ones with riches and wealth would use to make mergers so that the weaker of the two would not be taken over from the other through conquest. Wealth became the root of most marriages. Some marriages require what is known as a dowry, this is when the Groom is given a negotiated sum of money. Why do you need this if you love each other? Some couples spend billions on this ritual each year. How does it make sense to be in debt at the beginning of your future together? Why in some countries a man will burn his newly united wife with acid or pour alcohol on her and light a match, just because the family did not hold up on their end of the bargain? Why do a few women and a few men go through great lengths to marry U. S. soldiers around the world to have the privilege of virtually a tax free life or "The big PX in the sky"? Why do you find that young 20 year old end up with that 90 year old? These are just a few incidents to show just what marriage has become.

Love seems to not be part of the bargain today; women are trained subliminally that an agenda must be set and they set this agenda from what is known as the "Bio Clock". This is the point at which a woman cannot conceive when she reaches a certain age, and she gets the feeling that she has not contributed to society because she failed to give some male immortality through the exchange of genes.

They all want to be like little Cinderella's and wait for the day their prince will come to rescue them away. This is supposed to be the happiest time of your lives and you make it the most stressful. This is what society has made marriage for you as a woman and you don't have a clue what the meaning of it all means.

To men this is the beginning of the end and you have been given the burden of being the "bread winner" of your family. Some of you fall into the game of forcing your wife to stay at home and preform household duties until you get home. "Stupid Ass…" we lost that right years ago when we put the women to work outside the home; so you have to work twice as hard and you will die before can enjoy the fruits of your labor. Men feel that there is nothing to gain in marriage because a woman has a free ticket out whether she is faithful or not. Men feel: (That if she cheats she gets half if not all of my possessions if I cheat she gets the same and more.) Society has implanted that into our minds. Even if a prenuptial agreement is in place it still has the chance to be overturn if the circumstances permit.

In the past men and women unconditionally loved, later on couples wanted to celebrate and it was the religious groups that wanted you to make your vowels before GOD so that the marriage was more enriched. Some groups wanted to insure that that their women were untouched or a virgin so that they could have a pure path to the genes for conceiving children. All of this is stupid because when you love someone it does not matter what the situation is; because love is the reason we should get married not how it secures our future for capital gain. The promise is irrelevant because what time is compared to eternity and if you love; there is no end date to this. With true love you will never be bored. You will never know what emptiness is because your mate is in your heart. Love comes from the heart not the brain, the brain destroys love because it is illogical to act in it.

Think before you act. It's not a contract, licenses or status. Its love...

The secret to a good piece of good old fashion chocolate.

You've seen on TV many times how they go into the jungle and hunt down the Drug Cartel, they jump out of helicopters and these camouflage men are creeping in the woods and they sneak up to the compound they plot their targets and they give the team the signal and they spray the compound with bullets and wipe it out. They escape and they get back to the rendezvous point and the helicopter collects them and they come home the unsung heroes.

Well...

Why do they pass the chocolate harvester? Yes this is now most of the coca beans are brought to your shelves every day. Children are sold or stolen from their families and they are taken to a foreign land where they will spend the rest of their natural born live picking the coca pods and prepare them for harvesting. They are kept out of school and they start early in the morning and they work until the sun sets. They work with unsafe tools and if they are not careful, they can cut themselves with the machete. They will not be taken to a hospital or doctor. The Captors just work them until disease and infection set in (if the child is unlucky) then the child will chop and chop by force until they die on the spot.

All of this so you and your families can have the chocolate of your choice when you have a craving late in the day. They say that chocolate is a women's best friend. They say have a cup of hot chocolate when you are cold. They flood the market and it is everywhere.

My; how we love chocolate right? These children are put at the edge of villages and they sit there as these children watch other children grow up and have normal lives. Children who go to school, who have parents, and who play in the yard of these villages have fun while these children sit in the shadows. The sad part is that in most cases they do not know the native language of the region they are in. So they can't even cry for help or seek help. The parents in the village tell their children to stay away from them because these parents are scared or happy that their children do not suffer from the same fate.

We as society are nothing but consumers and we do not care where or how these goods get to us as long as it is convenient. When you look at that shirt or pair of shoes do you ever wonder where they come from? You waste precious goods and we are greedy to the core. We make ourselves blind to these issues because we always want the finial products. When you look at that tag and you see third world countries names have you really looked at the infrastructures of these regions? They will show you the state of the art facility so you can have a bit of comfort and you let this masquerade imbed in your mind.

What does death by chocolate mean to these children? The sad part is they have never tasted the very same chocolate they prepare for you to have in comfort.

What does this phrase mean to you?

Chocolate; sweet isn't it?

All of you are happy and you just let critical issues pass you by. You wake up in the morning, you get out of bed and you go to the refrigerator, you open it and you look for a glass of orange juice but it's not there. So you get a little grumpy and you continue on with your day, because you know that you will be able to pick some more up on your way to work. Its great isn't it?

Well what will you do when there was no more when you got to the store? As a matter of fact you get there and there is nothing at all. Where would you go, what would you do? What if today was the last day of your country as we know it? What would you do if your money were worth nothing to the world? What if today was the day your country became a third world country over night? What would you do if we can't buy any more oil? What would do if your lights go out? What would you do? When you walk down the street and cars are parked because there is no more gas, stores are empty because since we did not want encourage students to be producers instead of consumers?

We have no more mega grocery stores to run to when the refrigerator is empty. Keep thinking that these goods will always be there for your convenience and you will be lost when this day comes. Now you are in the second day that the shelves are empty. You have no reason to work because your job cannot afford to pay you. You still have a little faith that there is something out there you can do to survive. Wait; you hear something you look and what do you see? Yep that gas guzzling Sport Utility Vehicle (SUV) cruse down by with; yes you guessed it; the rich. You make it into town and you go to your favorite café to see if you can talk to your favorite cashier to see if they have any news on what is going on. You get to the door and you are stopped by two armed guards to your surprise. They tell you that you are not allowed to enter. You ask why and their replies are: "your kind is not allowed to enter" - not because you are black, not because you are white, it's because you are a lower class and you are beneath the new clients who are in the store and you won't fit in.

You turn away and you walk by the window and you look how they are wasting food and goods laughing at what they see outside. They laugh because they took their time to make you stupid, spoiled and unaware of what they had achieved for the final plan. The hunger starts to set in. What will you do? White collar jobs are not the answer to "the way to success". Yes it's an easy life and it pays good but blue collar jobs can be profitable as well.

This is why we have to let our children pursue their dreams no matter how silly they are. This is the difference between a thriving country and a third world country. We as society have lost this ethic and we are losing it fast. Give your children a chance to experience life and point out their strengths as well as their weakness. The rich don't want to embrace the family life because it's bad for business. That's why we work late hours and we live to work and not work to live.

People are kidnapped or sold for slavery just so you will never see an empty shelf. When you over produce you begin to waste products. You have no concept of the fundamentals of life. All you know is that it's not your problem and your fridge is full. Now you have graduates who walk into unemployment because there are too many in their field. You make the labor jobs uninviting and students have no encouragement to take them on and make them work. They are forced on them and all of that time for education is now lost.

The third day of your third world country; what will you do now?

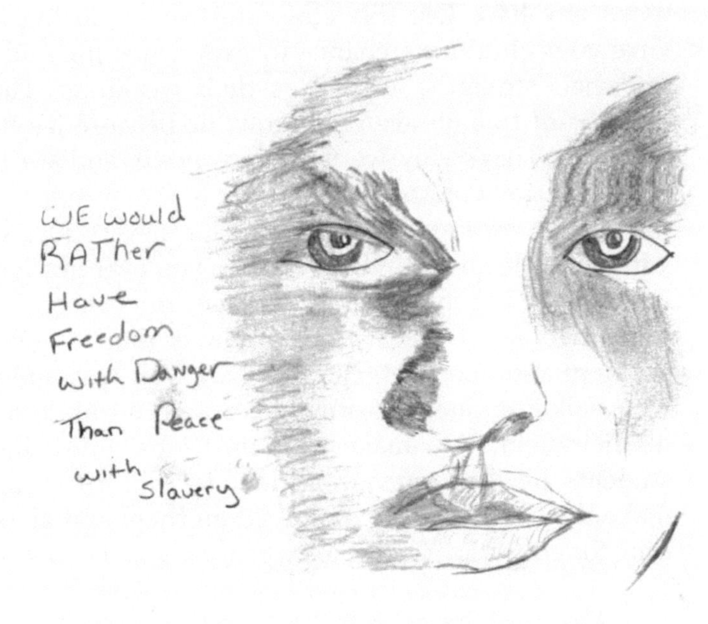

Give them a reason to be happy when they grow up.

We as society love the finer things in life. We want to have nice cars, nice cloths, nice jewelry and neat gadgets to play with. We want entertainment to make us feel satisfied when we go to sleep. We want it all and we will do everything in our power to have these things no matter what the cost. Well; there are people in society who want you to have these things as well but there is a twist to getting it to you. Children...

Yes children, they are sold, kidnapped, and brainwashed into giving these things for your so called comfort. How can you sleep at night knowing you directly or indirectly contribute to this business? Every day you passively walk by this problem and you let the madness go on. There are plenty of quality products that have and are produced under positively controlled sources. You never read the tag, you only read the logo. This is why you have such vast quantity of your goods to live with.

You sit idle while in your neighborhood and let that child preform sexual favors to the pedophiles of society. Just imagine these individuals spend vast amounts of money just to have a thrill. They do with what they want with children ages from infants to adolescents. Some of these people are so sick they demand to have has young as they can get because its better and it reduces their chance of have diseases. Little boys and girls who never knew how to spell sex, for the first time have to be bent over while some man three times their age thrust their penis into this child's anal or vaginal areas then after this man is finished the children are cleaned up so they can go to the next room where a woman three times their age is waiting and she forces these children to have oral sex and possible intercourse and the child has no idea why this is going on.

No country is immune to the sweat shop day after day these children are force to work under armed guards as they pump out the very same goods you buy off of the shelf. Some are malnourished others are beaten to death. They chain them to their work station and they are given a quota and if they do not meet this quota they are either beaten or they do not get to eat that day. They are tortured and yes murdered all for the sake of you being able to have the latest phone, latest fashion design, and that sparkling diamond. You never see the face of Inspector # 1,2,3,4. You never see made in a third world country, pick one they all practice this.

Just to wear the sparkling diamond a child is taken from his family forced to take up arms and massacre villages because greedy men want to own it all. They watch over other slaves as they are stripped searched before they leave the mine. These boys are given drugs and other substances to eases the night mares from their first kill. As they get a couple tours of duty they learn how to rape the women of these villages and murder them when they are done. When the conquest is over they are left in the dust to recover from what they have accomplished. They drive themself mad because they mostly never go home because they were forced to murder their on villages because they did not obey. Some of them get out and some of them become the next warlord because they know nothing else.

When they are finished with all of these types of slaves, they are murdered or dump out far away from their homes if they are lucky.

All of this so you can look good when you walk down the street.

Not your problem right?

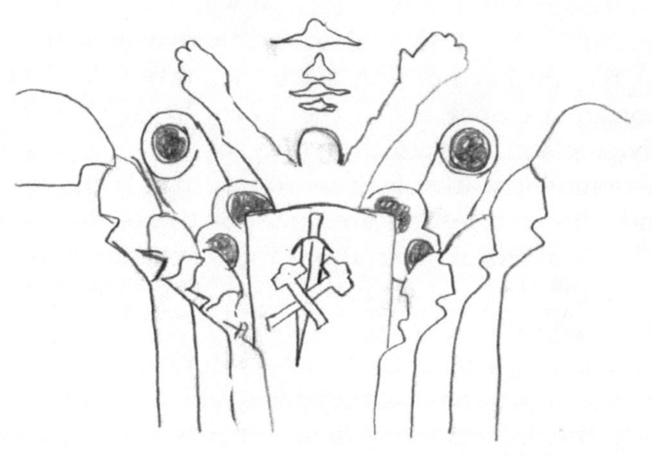

This has all of the potential to happen if you continue to live the way you do. They continue to show you nonsense on your TV's and play pointless music on your MP3 or radio. They show you movies with no vision. They show you your possible future and you are in a ruse and do not see what some artist have to say. You like the graphics or you love the beat. You never listen to the message and it sinks into your minds and you slowly become slaves to their way. They put beautiful things in your face but they do not give you a means to obtain it. They have got you to the point that you feel there is no other way to live and you must have better things in your life. Some of you are successful but you do not share your knowledge because you feel you will not get ahead. Why do you do this? Why can't we get there together?

It's sad but not only have they taken the lessons of managing money out of the school house they took out Civics class. This is the study of how your countries government works. Half of you do not even know how and who your leaders are. You don't know how they get into their offices. You also do not even know how they make the laws you complain about. They have got you so detached from your leaders that even if you vote you still do not have a pure say to who will take the office. They tax you to no end and they suckered you in to taxing not only the infrastructure and benefits, they tax you for making money and you deal with it. You pay millions and you only receive a fraction of what you put in.

You give away just about all of your rights and now you allow them to spy on you, arrest you or "detain" for 24 hours with no reason. They collect all sorts of information on you and you give it all to them through your favorite social network site. They basically keep you fat and stupid so they can move on with their agenda. It's funny that we are so free and we have laws that truly make no sense. It appears that you want this life because you are slowly letting slip out of your control. This is only possible because they keep the shelves full and your television on.

Well for those of you who don't know they added a new member to your government without your permission. They are called Lobbyist. These groups work for big organizations and they come to Washington DC to give your elected members in congress money. They make it sound better and I can think of nicer ways to tell you but that as real as it gets and to the point it can get.

They even have offices in your capital because they want to be right there when the laws are being made in their favor. Since you don't want the government to run correctly they participate in your government and they get to do whatever they want because you are too lazy to do the same. They operate with governments all over the world. This is possible because they kept you entertained so you destroy the middle class all by yourselves. You wonder why it's hard to get a job, you wonder why you bail out Banks that are too big to fail, and you wonder why billions of your hard earned money is given to CEO's for destroying your way of life. Well you let this all go on while you wanted to gather useless toys to play with.

The more passive you are the easier it is to lock you up in a cage and let the rich play and enjoy the freedom you were too lazy to preserve.

Is this your child's babysitter, teacher or both?

There was a time when the playground was the social meeting ground of the whole community. There was no doubt in any parent's mind where their children were. Such games as basketball, baseball and football occupied most of children's day. Parents knew the location of their children's whereabouts. Society has made this even easier for parents today with television; children now only go as far as the living room or den and now parents are with in ear shy of their child's activities now, but it comes with a cost.

Now children just sit there like drones viewing the "box of light" and the channel selection has increased; you need to be aware of what they are watching. It would be in your interest check in sometimes because censorship is slowly minimizing and this could be very surprising when you walk in on your child as they watch television or (TV). Try to introduce different activities for your child to get into so that they are not stuck in front of this system. TV has become a vital part the 21st Century and it can be helpful just as dangerous to your child's welfare. Children and some Adults believe whatever this device presents. You can see how it is dumbing your children down and you also can see the result of its progress; ask most children what they want to be when they grow up and you may be shocked.

TV producers like to show the rich and the famous life style and TV producers love to flaunt how others have it better then you. The sad part is that they never show you how they got there and you sit there as you watch this and you never truly ask yourself why. You fall into the traps of products that come on the commercials and your children run to you and you run to the store to feed this machine called Television. Yes you feed this machine like robots in the movie The Matrix. You forget why you have electricity, not because you need light to see in your house at night, it's because now you can't use your television most of all and that's not right.

TV is the corporation's biggest tool to get you to buy things in abundance and not out of necessity. This device has taught you how to be selfish to the ways of self and natural infrastructure.

Why do you need the newest model car when your car you have can last for years if you maintain it? Why do you have to go to the refrigerator when you are not even hungry? Why do you have to have the latest cellular phone when the phone you have works just fine.

Children are so lost in the concepts of TV propaganda, that they do not know the difference between reality and friction. You think it is good that your child is doing fine in the other room this is scary because we as adults forget that our children are like sponges picking a surface of liquid. When you observe or you hear or see your child do things which are totally alien to your house hold, you have to wonder. Think of where they have been sitting for the last 4 hours of the afternoon. Yes this could be where a large percentage of their actions may have come from.

You as a parent can change this; activate the parental controls which are provided for you. This is what the rich do because they want to preserve their riches. If you ever have the chance to ask a rich person if they let their children watch TV. The majority of them will tell you that they do not let them watch TV. Actors ironically when interviewed will also proudly say that their children watch little to no TV. When you look at the majority of the rich people's homes you almost never see the TV. Only the newly found fortune finders home have TV but it is not connected to the network. Funny how they give you the secrets to success and you listen more to the advertisement then the information. Take the time to cut off the TV and give your child a book. Take the time to play a game of monopoly. Share some of your triumphs and failures, start slowly you don't have to go "cold turkey" there are a lot of channels with good information.

TV steals from imagination but a book enhances it.

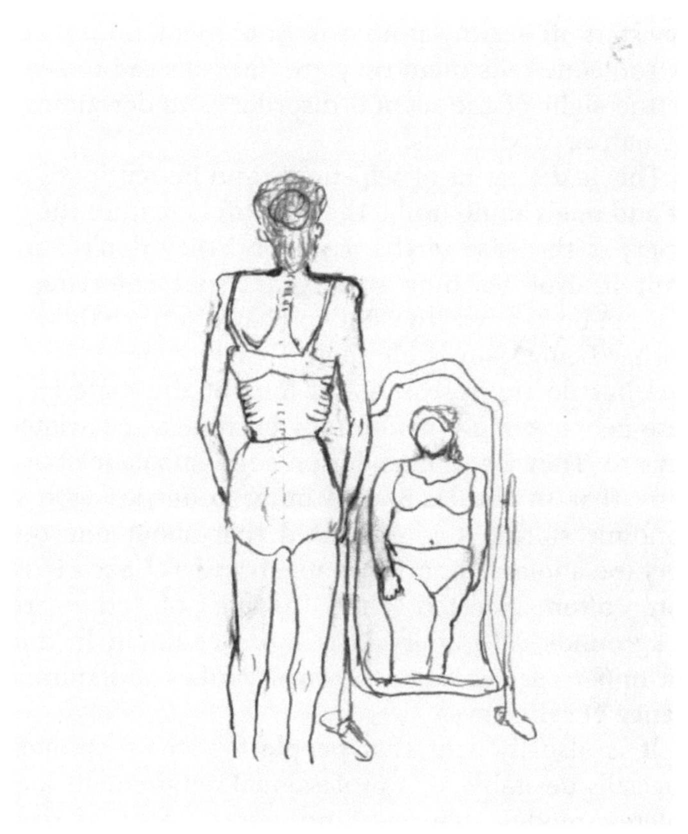

This is a product of Society and this we should be ashamed of. These people and others like them fear food. This is because when they look in the mirror and they feel that they are extremely overweight. They spend their days starving themselves because the world in their minds thinks they are more than average in their weight sizes.

They start off healthy at lease most of them, until that one day someone tells them they are "fat". It's sad to see this but the sight of the mental disorder is undermining the true nature of what it is.

This is the result of selfishness and insecurity of one's self and one's ability to be the beautiful creature they are. Society is the base of this issue and they don't want to admit it. Not teaching society and not enforcing true values to be happy with what you have; you see the effects of what being vain is all about. I may sound mean and cruel but do the research and look at the material that these people endure before they become as emaciated as they are. They try to blame it on gene imbalance but it is funny that In the U. S. and other countries with high economic status, it is estimated that about one out of every 100 adolescent girls has the disorder. Caucasians are more often affected than people of other racial backgrounds, and anorexia is more common in middle and upper socioeconomic groups. Makes you think is it science or selfishness.

It is also thought that people for whom thinness is especially desirable, or a professional requirement such as athletes, models, dancers, and actors, to be at risk for eating disorders such as anorexia nervosa. Wow you find most of these people on TV right? So in theory; subliminally you contribute to this issue and you don't even know it. When you fight to get into that size less than your original size think about it; there is someone trying harder then you. We do not like these issues but they are just parts of our society we who shelves are always full never see.

There are possibilities that this situation can be cured because people bounce back. Why this is possible is because the people who help these individuals teach them that they are worth it to be whom they are. When you live in a society that is based on accumulation and hording of goods derivatives like this become the outcome.

People never want to learn anything new because they are always happy with complacency. This is why we have issues that we have today. People like to get the wooden spoon, the belt or the stick just to learn simple values. Why is it that our societies allow people to get this far when it can be cared for months before it comes to this? Well it all goes back to finance and health care that refuses to address these issues. There are doctors and specialist out there waiting to help these people but as you see insurance and health care's laws wait until the last minute to do something about it. They wait until that one story that shocks the world appears and that's when they jump through hoops to address issues such as this.

The only reason they can refer to this disorder to societies like ours because the third world countries are always starving and most places they look like this because of war and strife. You have to get out of the bubble and see just what is going on around you. Take the time to discover your unknowns; it helps you to address the pre-symptoms of or society to be addressed. In due time, we humans can be salvaged from this behavior.

Teach our society the importance of self-preservation
and to not be scared of a plate of food.

Are you sure you want to privatize this institution as well?

This is another reason to pay attention to your country and its actions. Prisons are the new up and coming investment prospect of America and it may not be a pretty site in the end. The U. S. government loves to out source and as you noticed it is always awarded to the lowest bidder. Well once you take this instution and privatize it you may open a can of worms you do not want to go fishing with. Prisons are the methods that our government uses to consolidate convicts for rehabilitation. Though some methods are not in some cases humaine to most; the government can sill control how these institutions will be managed. Well due to you allowing your government to out source and send jobs overseas. People get kicked out of jobs and soon start to figure out ways to feed their families. The corporations knew this and they layed the foundation for this instution to be out sourced as well.

Just imagine if one of these corporations where to have finincial hardships? Think of what they are doing with business today and how they are cutting employees or cutting products on the shelf because they do not sell? Now imagine what type of cuts will be conducted when the Prison Corporation is having a hardship? This could lead to some interesting issues for the future. Issues like mass executions without further appeals. Or worse they will let what they consider not so life threating crimes like rape or pedophilia or the drug seller and the drug user and give them freedom. You can run to the government but they will just tell you that this is a private corporation decision and they are protected by The Better Bussiness Bureau. What if they have to cut prison guards? This is a good potential for prison riots. You say that there will be plenty of funds to support but what happens when the prison corporation becomes too big to fail? You guess it you the tax payer will have to pay for an institution you already paid for in the past with better standards. Then of course they bring in cheap labor say from the many third world countries we support and the up and coming super power China. Have you seen what their prisons look like? If you did it would make you cringe. They have the potential to resort to all sorts of measures to make money even sell body parts to the international market just to play with a theory. Relax you don't have to worry as long as you don't break the law you will be ok right.

Are you sure? "As I've said before; corporation right?" As you know what comes with corporations come the lobbyist. Yes the good old lobbyist, who wants to make profits, will go to Washington DC and pay off; you guessed it, that representative or senator; to turn misdemeanors into felonies and the game is on. Now cops can put you in jail for crimes like parking tickets and J walking. That will be fun right? Cops even now can apprehend you without reason for 24 hours at any time weather they suspect you are not. This is a long time to beat you to a pulp or plant enough evidence to get you into these corporations such as this one you see now. Look at the measures that the government has taken to bring this institution to life. Look around at the crimes how more and more they are finding ways to bring you in. Look how arrest rates are on the rise in the U. S. today; it's all around you and soon you will fall into the trap and resort to your passiveness until it's too late.

Just remember; when it says corporation you can always bet that 99. 9% it is a business; and when times get hard for a business they begin to cut jobs; or figure out ways to bring the money in to stay in business. If you are happy with the way things are just wait I think you will not have the same opinion when this starts to affect you later down the line. We already got rid of the car industry; we already got rid of the retail market, now they are working to get rid of the prison market. This has a much greater financial potential then the others because people love to make babies and some babies love to get into trouble. Also the more money you have the easier it will be to keep out of prison.

Yep business is money and they don't care where it is coming from. Break the law in the future and you may not have any rights to stand on.

What ever happen to letting children dream? Why do
you hold your child back? Why is it so hard to let them
fall out of the nest and you insist to keep them under your
wing? Parents these days have forgotten how to let their
children grow in a well-rounded way. Yes we love our
children and they are precious in every way but keep in
mind that too much protection and too much negative
persuasion can be unhealthy and in the end you pay the
price.

Understand that you cannot walk in the path of your children shoes when they walk out the door they are bombarded with all sorts of personalities and influences. Some are good and some are bad. Some of them will agree to and some of them will not. This is your child's first step to individualism and you owe it to them to have this and build it in their own way. As long as you work with your children and not against them they will build a character we can live with. You do not have to always spank them to get your point across and society will not let you because they want your child to be a spoiled brat because it feeds the economy. Now it seems like the children are the parents and the parents are the kids. You let this happen ever since you let your government's social youth services interfere with your family life.

Take the time to be a part of your children's life and you will find there is a lot of new ideas you can use yourself; let them explore that uncharted territory. Let them get a bump or two on the way. Sheltering children from life is dangerous to their personality and there awareness. Children in the past were adventurous and now they are what I call house rats. Due to this they slowly lose a lot of knowledge which will not be found in most books. Most of them don't even know how to fix a broken chain on a bike. When I was a boy it was uncommon to not know how to use a football, a baseball, a soccer ball and a tennis ball. Now a child only knows these items from video games and television. Sad isn't it?

Keep this up children will be too lazy to make your country the proud place you knew it as. When you hold back their dreams you hold back the potential of them becoming productive citizens. When you hold them back you lose the chance of having the best that humanity has to offer. You laugh at this but that same laugh is why you are broke and you don't own your own land and you live from check to check trying to make ends meet. You can't see the potential you had in yourself and now you try to give this same negativity to your child. You are stuck in your conservative ways keeping your child back and this stands in the way. What ever happen to the mother of invention? This is what we had when we were children? We were always in the back yard doing something. This led to the astronauts, the captains of ships, the jet pilots we know today. As children we used our brothers and sisters our cats and dogs as patients so we could become doctors and veterinarians. We explored the back woods in our neighborhoods which led to the treasure hunters of today. The world you live in today at your comfort was built from children whose parents let them grow like trees and not like cactuses.

Hold your children back and you miss out on your own fortune. Just because you did not have it good, when you grew up, this is no reason to steal this from your children. Give your child the chance to pursue their dreams and regardless of the case, the parents normally win. Like I said in the beginning you take care of your children they take care of you. Don't miss out on the treasures your child will come upon. It's not about money or fame because if they find a cure for a deadly disease or they make contributions to knowledge we all win. In some cases even some street thugs never bothered the child with the scholarship, because they knew that this child was going to be someone who they could say represented something good to redeem all of the faults the thugs have committed.

If they see it, why don't you?

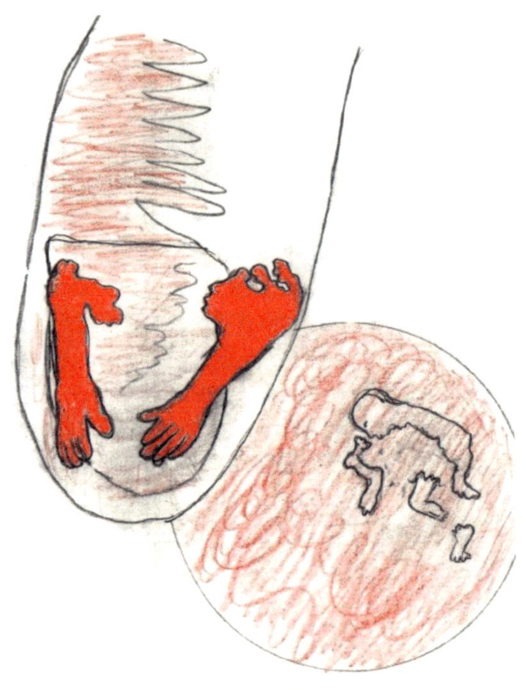

These hands could have done a lot of good. These hands could have done a lot of wrong. Unfortunately they will never have a chance to do anything because they were sucked out of a selfish mother because it was not convenient for her to have these hands at this point in her life. These hands could have been the next president.

These hands could have been the next dictator. Unfortunately these hands will never have a chance to be either because a father was too scared to help that mother out with these hands when come out. These hands could have been the symbol of peace. These hands could have been the symbol of war. Unfortunately these hands will never have the chance because a father and a mother did not practice safe sex so these hands can come at a later date. These hands could have cured a deadly disease. These hands could have created a biological epidemic. Unfortunately these hands will never have a chance because a mother's family found it not fitting to have these hands because of a family's honor that these hands could have disgraced. These hands could have built the first abundant energy source. These hands could have destroyed the last bit of energy we have. Unfortunately these hands will never have a chance to do this because some father's parents did not want to be grandparents at an early age. These hands could have discovered a new star. These hands could have discovered the meteorite which will be our doom. Unfortunately these hands will not have the chance because a mother was scared the children would laugh at her at school. These hands could have reached mars and beyond. These hands could have found Atlantis. Unfortunately these hands will never have a chance because a mother and a father did not want to destroy a marriage they did not enjoy with their other. These hands could have been you. These hands could have been me. Fortunately my hands can type this story because my parents cared for me.

This is the result of society when they fail to teach younger children the value of life and the fundamentals of values. This can be prevented and it can be controlled but religion, money, and no education is the result of this.

People just do not see the result of this because the health professionals in this field who perform this act do not want to show you the result of what you have done. This is hard to see but this goes on in the world. Society hides this practice and people think it is ok. You have circumstances where this can in societies eyes be beneficial but those acts were happening long before us and they gave these hands a chance to change the world. The humans who lived of the past took life just as fast as they made it. The difference is that the humans in the past gave these hands a chance to seal their fate.

All you have to do is take the extra measures before you get into your groove and take the steps so you can give these hands a chance to change the world. Society has once again made it normal to take the opportunity to steal this away from these hands. What gives us the power to take the life away from these hands? What you fail to realize is that when you decide to steal the chance from these hands, you take the chance to never have another set of hands again. Yes; some women who have a bad experience with their abortion due to the fault of the person doing the procedure destroys the woman's uterus and therefore the women can never have the chance to have children again. Some mothers even die during the procedure and we all lose.

Stop running away from your problems. Children are gifts from our God - no matter whom you are and who your god is.

Give these hands a chance to change the world - no matter what the circumstance.

Well you got past this book because you made it here. I hope that I was able to open new avenues of thinking. Please don't get mad at the messenger, get mad at society and set it straight. You have seen just a few episodes of the life and acts around you. You have the power to change the world. You should stop sitting by and just letting it all crumble from beneath your feet.

To all of the ones who are out there making this knowledge accessible thank you; it was a pleasure to receive the knowledge that is presented in my book. I hope you will not be afraid to crawl out of the tunnels and enjoy the horizon of knowledge.

If you are upset I beg you to prove me wrong. Prove that the word is coming together and we are truly fixing our problem. Prove that we are striving to be better societies, prove that children can all have good quality lives. Prove that People are working to bring back our societies to a standard we can live with. I am not talking about one are two issues that you use to generalize the millions of issues we have. I want you to prove that there are true solutions to true problems that are menacing our world today.

If you think this is impossible; then you have a lot to learn and work on.

Since this will not happen in a day I will have another book coming soon. This was just to try a new and different way of seeing things that most do not like to talk about. Get out of your shell, strive for knowledge, educate yourselves because the world will not.

Learn what is going on and learn how to succeed in life and don't give up. Its not over because you can turn it all around and make it better.

Being that you made it to the end you have proven that you seek knowledge and you want to persue the "what if's" in your life. I am sure you may have a lot of questions, this is your chance to search for the knowledge you seek. Yes you may think positive or negative thoughts and you are surely welcome to this. I am sure most of you will have your say and this is nice. No matter what your opinion is talk about it, let the world know your personal opinion on this book. I will not be mad at you. Heck if you see me, cuss me out or congratulate me. Just remember, if this touched you in such a way, this means it worked and you have taken the first step re-buliding the culture we are letting fade away.

If you keep your feelings in, then well you will be the demise of your doom. You will continue to be the drones and uneducated I discused in this book. Society will use you and abuse you and when the real problems begin, you will eather become a slave to survive; or you will die because you could not grow in the knowledge you walk away from.

Get mad, get happy, but most of all get smart...

Thank you.